KEN WORPOLE was born in 1944 in Derbyshire—to which the Hackney Mothers' Hospital had been evacuated during the war. He attended primary school in East London and later in Essex. At sixteen he left school and for the next five years worked as a site clerk with various building and civil engineering companies throughout Britain, before deciding to become a teacher. Trained as a mature student, he taught English in a Hackney comprehensive until 1973, when he left to set up the Centerprise local publishing project in Hackney, East London.

Ken Worpole has taught evening classes in Hackney for the past fourteen years, mostly under the auspices of the Workers' Educational Association. He is also involved in the Federation of Worker Writers and Community Publishers, a voluntary body that links working-class writers' workshops and local publishing initiatives in Britain. He has published many articles on the teaching of English, British working-class history and on cultural politics in *The New Statesman, New Society, Times Educational Supplement* and *New Left Review*. He has edited, with Dave Morley, *The Republic of Letters* (1982), a collection of essays on working-class writing.

Married with two chldren, Ken Worpole lives in Hackney and has recently returned to teaching.

Ken Worpole

Verso

Dockers and Detectives

Popular Reading: Popular Writing

© Ken Worpole 1983

Verso Editions
15 Greek Street London W1V 5LF

Filmset in Plantin by
Comset Graphic Designs

Printed by
The Thetford Press Ltd,
Thetford, Norfolk

ISBN 0 86091 079 2
　　　0 86091 779 7

Contents

For
The Members Of
The Federation of Radical Booksellers

Introduction

All of these studies have their origins in conversations with other people, conversations about books and reading. We have talked in the kinds of settings where people often do talk about books and ideas: at family gatherings, in pubs after meetings, on trains or while driving from one place to another, or when I have interviewed people in their homes. 'But surely you've read...', 'When I was young, you know, we all used to read...' 'Now there's a book that made a great impression on me....' The studies in this book may appear to intellectualize those reading patterns, those individual reminiscences, those dozens of separate titles and publication dates, into a pattern of highly personal interpretation. I have been conscious of this happening, but could not avoid it. In order to make sense of the past in the light of contemporary crises in the popular culture of reading and writing, I have had to take down all those books from where they were randomly located on the shelves and sort them crudely into piles according to the integrating principle of a historical theme.

These studies are attempts at cultural reconstruction, of some particular patterns of reading and writing during the past fifty years that conventional literary criticism has ignored. They owe as much to what I have learned from talking to other people as they do to sitting in the Reading Room at the British Museum tracking down books whose authors or titles—and sometimes both—had been forgotten, but which people at some moment thought had been important. So often, while doing this, I was struck by the amount of valuable, lively and powerful work that had been allowed to sink into obscurity, work which could still come alive again if republished, and I know that other people also engaged in this kind of historical re-reading feel much the same. Feminist publishing has shown the way forward, in its recovery of past texts that orthodox commercial publishing had allowed to fall into obscurity. The fragmentation of working class historical and cultural consciousness now fiercely debated by such writers as Eric Hobsbawm, Stuart Hall, and particularly Jeremy Seabrook, is not exactly surprising given the fragmentation and lack of concern for the material artefacts of that consciousness, that is to say the photographs, short stories, novels, autobiographies, histories produced by that historical class culture which were allowed to disappear through neglect, or were killed at the roots by recurring frosts of socialist economism. The banners were allowed to go mouldy because they were old-fashioned; the trade-union branch minutes or party records were burnt because they were just more old paper; the photographs got lost; the poems, stories, novels and autobiographies weren't kept in print because it wasn't 'economic'; the buildings fell into neglect because it wasn't really important where people met, since one place was as good as another. Such processes were not actively resisted, yet people are surprised that 'consciousness' has become 'discontinuous'.

The basis of any kind of literature is economic. Only a fraction of the books written are published, and only a fraction of those published are promoted and distributed in popular and interventionist ways. It may well be that the books people most compulsively want to read actually have not been written or produced, let alone published (the development of non-commercial local publishing in Britain over the past ten years has created significantly large numbers of new readers for forms of writing that have conventionally been felt to be coterie interests, such as poetry, local history, dialect writing and autobiography). What people *want to read* and what they are *able to buy* are two separate things though the bestseller lists cannot encompass that distinction. As long as the cultural production of, particularly, literature and history remains part of general capitalist production we cannot possibly get the range of literature and history that a cultural democracy would expect. Nevertheless, the fact that so many millions of books continue to be published and read does testify to capitalism's ability to seem to respond to people's cultural needs (as it sometimes actually does, of course). We cannot dismiss popular literature, genre fiction, and popular history as produced within a commercial framework as simply 'escapist' or 'diversionary' reading.

What makes popular literature popular? This is the question we need to ask. And having asked the question, a concern for popular cultural production requires that we build on what we have learned in order to develop and transcend the forms and achievements to which capitalist production has accustomed us, but which it cannot take any further because it doesn't, finally, have a direct relationship with the people who read and write the books it publishes, other than that of the cash nexus. One lesson we ought to learn from the 1930s is that you cannot criticize your way out of a cultural crisis: you have to supplant it. This is what to a large extent happened in the 1930s when the working class movement responded to the inability of capitalist cultural production to meet felt needs by developing its own film-making, theatre-making, photographic and documentary recording projects as well as socialist publishing initiatives.

That commercial publishing can only approximate to people's needs is quite obvious, particularly to those, who like myself have worked in education and small scale non-commercial publishing projects over the past decade. For when oppositional educational movements have identified new reading constituencies, such as that for working class autobiography, or for adult literary work, or for young black writers, they have been able to respond to these needs directly—and in co-operation with the readers themselves—whereas commercial publishing has usually floundered in a sea of stereotyped thinking, anachronistic imagery and the paucity of detail which always comes with the commercial need for generalization. And it is a feature of contemporary publishing that the commercial publishers now follow where oppositional movements lead and innovate. No new publisher's catalogue is complete without its Social History, Black Studies and Feminist sections. Yet they cannot create these literatures, only hover around the movements which actually do create them, and try to buy these texts second-hand. In this they follow the pattern of the wider process of capitalist intellectual production which Hans Magnus Enzensberger has aptly described:

> The mind industry can take on anything, digest it, reproduce it, and pour it out. Whatever our minds can conceive of is grist to its mill; nothing will leave it unadulterated: it is capable of turning any idea into a slogan and any work of the imagination into a hit. This is its overwhelming power, yet it is also its most vulnerable spot: it thrives on a stuff which it cannot manufacture by itself. It depends on the very substance it must fear most, and must suppress what it feeds on: the creative productivity of people.[1]

Yet still so little of the left's resources have been utilized to aid and encourage this creativity, almost as if it were scared to face the problems of production, and preferred the safer role of criticizing popular consumption. Despite the lack of any real support from the wider 'labour movement', working class writing is currently flourishing, though in forms different from that of the 1930s and earlier periods of popular literary activity. And reading itself continues to flourish despite predictions of 'the end of the book' and the decline of reading habits. Too much talk of endings forecloses the idea of new possibilities. A proverb used in my family to revive optimism still encourages me: As one door closes, somewhere another one opens.

There are many people to thank for help with this book, directly and indirectly. Naming names is an invidious activity and I am bound to omit through lapse of memory or oversight the names of some of the most important people who have encouraged me, to whom I apologize in advance. The list is long but these people helped write this book and so deserve some authorial credit: Alexander Baron, Dave Barnes, Eddie Barratt, Neil Belton, Ian Bild, Philip Corrigan, Andy Croft, Jack Dash, Mike Davis, Jerry Dawson, Bob Drewer, John Field, Gerry Gregory, James Hanley, John Hampson, Maggie Hewit, Bill Keal, Jean Milloy, Roger Mills, Rebecca O'Rourke, Alan O'Toole, Dave Pearson, Olive Rogers, Raphael Samuel, Barbara Shane, Sue Shrapnel, Jerry White, Larraine Worpole and Eileen and Stephen Yeo.

The mistakes and idiosyncracies of interpretation are all mine.

Ken Worpole

1
Fictional Politics:
Traditions and Trajectories.

People are not linked to the past exclusively by the historical associations of the material culture in which they live. They also inherit intellectual and moral patterns of belief, certain kinds of political and cultural understanding, which though invisible, possess a dogged power of their own. The cluster of traditions surrounding people's relationships to books, genres of writing, and the activity of reading itself, remains, I believe, largely unexamined. There are literally thousands of books in print concerning the teaching of reading—and less than a handful make any reference whatsoever to the social history of this activity, or to the cultural difficulties that continue to be brought to bear upon the acquisition of this skill. The contemporary reading public and its reading preferences are analyzed with regard to book distribution, price, genre, promotion and accessibility; every factor is taken into consideration except possibly the most important one of all, the divided and embattled cultural history of the very activity itself—reading. All questions of cultural politics are, in the first instance, historical questions.

Fiction: Unrespectable Writing

The novel in England had its origins in the popular culture of criminal ballads and the street literature of London's underworld or *demi-monde*. As Lennard J. Davis summarizes it in his excellent study, *Factual Fictions: The Origins of the English Novel*:

> The frequency with which the early English novel, newspaper and ballads focused on the criminal is significant. There seems to have been something inherently novelistic about the criminal, or rather the form of the novel seems almost to demand a criminal content. Indeed, without

the appearance of the whore, the rogue, the cutpurse, the cheat, the thief, or the outsider it would be impossible to imagine the genre of the novel.[1]

It is not surprising, therefore, that from the start there should have been prohibitive criticism of the genre. This linked the reading of such fiction with a criminal influence upon the reader's own behaviour. Davis's study cites many of these early objections, and cites also the defensive prefaces written by early novelists assuring the reader that their aim in portraying the criminal underworld was to finally show how such characters all came to an unhappy end or reformed their behaviour. Even so, since the very concept of 'fictionality' was then hardly formalized, many early novel-readers assumed that what they were reading was in fact true. And in the formulae used by authors to preface their novels, there was also a suggestion that the writer had simply relayed a story as told to him or her, based on actual events. Until the 1724 Stamp Act, 'a turning point in the history of the press and consequently of the novel'[2] most broadsheet or magazine publications hardly ever distinguished the factual from the fictional; what are wholly distinct categories of writing for us today were then part of a single literary discourse. The Stamp Act unintentionally forced publishers to distinguish the two since the Act put a tax on news and left all other forms of writing untaxed. Yet the ambiguity about the reality of what is told in fictional writing, an ambiguity upon which the very form of the novel is predicated, actually remains with us today.

This is not simply an effect of the discourse of fiction itself; it is also connected to the phenomenal and almost mesmeric quality of the printed word. Another historian of the early English novel, Ian Watt, wrote that:

> The authority of print—the impression that all that is printed is necessarily true—was established very early. If Autolycus's ballads were in print, Mopsa was 'sure they are true'. The innkeeper in Don Quixote had the same conviction about romances.[3]

A.E. Dobbs in his study *Education and Social Movements*[4] recounts the story of Stephen Knowles, 'a miner dwelling at Grassington...a collector of chap-books, who believed what he read. "It is not likely," he argued, "that anyone would go to the expense of printing lies."'

This belief could still be found in a fundamental form in our own century, as evidenced in a recent South Wales autobiography, *Rhymney Memories* by Thomas Jones:

> ...my father saw in a shop window a book called *The History of Tom Jones* by Henry Fielding. He was intrigued and went in and bought it for eighteen pence vowing he would read it. He never did, as he quickly fell asleep over a long book but my mother read it. She believed every word of it and could not conceive how a man could sit down and invent the story of Squire Allworthy and Sophia and Tom out of his head. So did Robert Owen before her read *Robinson Crusoe* and Richardson's novels and believe every word to be true. But my mother was fifty before she read a novel and to her dying day she had not completely grasped the nature of fiction or drama. The then current attitude is well shown by this sentence from a contemporary lecture by a leading Welsh preacher and Doctor of Divinity: 'Novels, the disgrace of English literature, and the curse of multitudes of English readers, do not take with Welsh readers.'[5]

The writer was talking about beliefs and attitudes still to be found in the 1920s—some 200 hundred years after the factual/fictional discourses were formally and generically distinguished—which shows how resilient such religious and cultural patterns of belief and understanding can be.

The culture of reading also has a particular history of gender relations associated with it. Ian Watt's account of the early novel and its readership details the process by which the new circulating libraries, and the writers themselves, regarded the woman reader as the principal component of the reading public then. Writing about the first half of the 18th century when the novel was establishing itself as a significant literary form, Watt comments:

> The distribution of leisure in the period supports and amplifies the picture already given of the composition of the reading public; and it also supplies the best evidence available to explain the increasing part in it played by women readers. For, while many of the nobility and gentry continued their cultural regress from the Elizabethan courtier to Arnold's 'Barbarians', there was a parallel tendency for literature to become a primarily feminine pursuit.[6]

Another reason for the gender of the early novel-reading public was that here was a form in which women were early contributors, possibly even founders. In Davis's more recent study of the early novel, he criticizes Watt and other historians of the genre for overlooking what was possibly the formative period of the novel before Defoe, to be found in the popular romances of such women writers as Aphra Behn, Mrs Manly, Mary Davys, Eliza Haywood and others.[7]

The gender relationship was simultaneously a class relationship. In the 18th century the novel-reading public was located firmly within the monied and leisured middle and upper classes. As the novel began to separate out into different genres—romantic, picaresque, Gothic, historical—it became much less gender-specific, although the romantic novel, whose origins in Britain go back conventionally to Richardson's *Pamela* and thus make it one of the most established of the fictional genres, along with the picaresque novel, has retained almost exclusively a female readership. And from its origins to the present day the novel has been one of the few cultural forms in which women have been able to attain some real dominance, though at times they have had to disguise their gender in order to do so, as in the case of Mary Ann Evans, most commonly known as George Eliot.

A third significant inter-connection for our purposes has been that of reading with religiosity. 'Protestantism,' as Halévy once wrote, is a 'book religion'.[8] In his UNESCO survey of contemporary international publishing, *The Book Revolution*, Robert Escarpit looked back to the first mass movements based on enlarging and capturing the reading public:

> In the last third of the eighteenth century, trends of thought which though at variance with one another, all converged in the direction of spreading books among what was then called "the people"—Methodism in England, Encyclopaedism and later, the revolutionary spirit in France, and, to a lesser extent, *Aufklärung* in Germany—suddenly made the need for reading matter an urgent problem.[9]

There was always a strong distrust—within non-conformist religions particularly—of imaginative literature. Richard Altick's indispensable study of the 18th and 19th century reading publics summarizes this pervasive religious distrust, whilst admitting that the subject deserves a lengthy study in its own right, a study which remains as yet unaccomplished.

For the evangelical denominations had a passionate suspicion of imaginative literature: a suspicion which fatefully determined the reading experience of millions of people during the whole century. This neo-Puritan proscription of literature which did not directly enrich its readers' Christian character had so far-reaching an effect upon English culture that it deserves thorough treatment in a separate book.[10]

Objections were made on several different grounds. A principal objection was on moral grounds: the characters in fiction inhabited a very secular world, in which they found happiness or otherwise through material or sensual gratification rather than through piety and self-denial. For the principal narrative ethic which underpinned the romance or the picaresque adventure was, of course, success and achievement in sexual love and material wealth, both in the world and most definitely of it. A second major objection was that reading fiction was time-wasting, time that would be better spent on good works, contemplation or direct religious activity.

These religious objections also carried over into the attitudes of many of the radical working-class movements as well. Richard Carlile, the intrepid and highly energetic 19th century radical publisher and bookseller described himself as 'an implacable enemy of all fiction, allegory, personification and romance.' Despite many periods of imprisonment during the 'war of the unstamped press' in the early part of that century, it does seem likely that given the opportunity Carlile might well have become a quite ruthless censor himself, given his remarks on the popular fiction of the time: 'Everything of this kind should now go into the fire. He who burns a romance purifies the human mind.'[11]

It is possible to see how both the evangelical and radical distrust affected people deeply by glancing at the career of one 19th-century working class-radical, George Howell, about whom we have a reasonably detailed biography by F.M. Leventhal based on Howell's own letters and reminiscences.[12] Leventhal wrote of Howell's early years of self-education:

> Although familiar with Wordsworth and Byron by this time, Howell continued to avoid Shakespeare until he obtained the reluctant approval of his Methodist class leader, whose suspicion of imaginative literature reflected conventional Evangelical attitudes.[13]

In one of his diary entries—in 1859, while still working as a foreman in the London building trade—Howell describes how he secured a ticket to the British Museum Reading Room, an honour and a privilege he thought would be betrayed by using it to read 'any work of fiction or general literature.' Moral reservations shade into what was by then an equally censorious utilitarian attitude towards fiction, an attitude less concerned with spiritual dilution than with the fact that imaginative literature produced no direct and measurable benefits to those who read it. Such literature contributed nothing to material progress, unlike works of useful knowledge, encyclopaedias and other forms of self-education and self-improvement. So while Howell was expressing an Evangelical guilt about the reading of fiction, Jeremy Bentham and the Utilitarians were also inveighing against such writing which distracted people from the more serious business of the pursuit of happiness.[14]

Ironically, when William Morris came to write his utopian novel *News From Nowhere* a generation later—profoundly anti-utilitarian though he was in most respects—his feelings about fiction echoed those of the utilitarians and the evangelicals. For in the novel, the young woman Clara who represents all that is best in the new socialist commonwealth is shown admonishing her grandfather for his old-fashioned and pre-revolutionary hankering after books to read:

> As for your books, they were well enough for times when intelligent people had but little else in which they could take pleasure and when they must needs supplement the sordid miseries of their own lives with imaginations of the lives of other people. But I say flatly that in spite of all their cleverness and vigour, and capacity for story-telling, there is something loathsome about them. Some of them, indeed, do here and there show some feeling for those whom the history books call 'poor', and of the misery of whose lives we have some inkling; but presently they give it up, and towards the end of the story we must be contented to see the hero and heroine living happily in an island of bliss on other people's troubles; and that after a long series of sham troubles (or mostly sham) of their own making, illustrated by dreary introspective nonsense about their feelings and aspirations, and all the rest of it; while the world must even then have gone on its way, and dug and sewed and baked and built and carpentered round about these useless animals.

That Morris himself had some sympathy with these sentiments, even if he didn't share them entirely, seems fairly conclusive. The diatribe against 'dreary introspective nonsense about their feelings and aspirations' is of a piece with Morris's own antagonism to the modernist literature of his own time, his dislike of Ibsen, for instance. The new concern with exploring the individual psyche and focusing on the more subjective forms of human alienation did not appeal to Morris, in whose own long narrative poems and prose works individual subjective states are pushed aside in the excessive attention to social activity and the emphasis on the physical constraints of life and labour. The notion that mental well-being waited directly upon physical well-being, and that the communism of property would automatically usher in an end to mental distress, was not, in retrospect, a particularly useful contribution to socialist theory. In other formulations it became a deliberate philistinism, or economism, a ruthless dismissal of the many personal and expressive forms of cultural exchange and popular self-activity.

Traces and echoes of these different attitudes to reading, and particularly the reading of fiction, actually do still exist. In discussions in evening classes, in conversations with librarians and bookshop workers, it is still the case that quite a number of people continue to hold strong reservations about the value, whether moral or utilitarian, of reading fiction. Biographies and histories, travel books and documentary books, it is argued, are far more interesting than fiction and they are 'real'. Other people continue to see reading as a quietist, even anti-social activity. Without an understanding of the complex history of these deeply held attitudes and beliefs, most comment on popular reading patterns ends up (as it does in so much educational pedagogy and books about literacy) in a strident and class-bound moralism.

Working-class reading

Despite its tradition of passivity, one of the great strengths of the British working-class socialist movement has been its keen interest in literature and other forms of imaginative writing. The general studies of the 19th century working class reading public, such as those of Altick, Wickwar, Webb, James, Neuberg and Simons[15] continually attest to this phenomenon. Then there is Engels's memorable famous passage in *The Condition of the English Working Class*:

> I have often heard working-men, whose fustian jackets scarcely hold together, speak upon geological, astronomical, and other subjects, with more knowledge than most 'cultivated' bourgeois in Germany possess.

> And in how great measure the English proletariat has succeeded in attaining an independent education is shown especially by the fact that the epoch-making products of modern philosophical, political, and poetical literature are read by working-men almost exclusively.

One suspects that there has never been any great problem in the past about a division between 'popular' and 'serious' literature and that most people have moved easily between the two, as they continue to do today. The early 19th-century radical Samuel Bamford was from an early age intoxicated by the lurid chap-book stories he found for sale in a local printer's shop.[16] In the early part of this century, Harry McShane admits to an early liking for 'bloods', 'stories about Sweeney Todd and Dick Turpin with people cutting throats and trap-doors and stuff like that.'[17] Neither found it difficult to develop more sophisticated tastes or remain eclectic readers throughout their lives. The rigid demarcation line that separates 'popular' and 'serious' writing is a product of a class culture—and its many institutions, particularly the universities—which resist all attempts to widen cultural democracy. By erecting large walls around a select number of approved texts, 'the canon', 'the great tradition', they both prevent any possibility of literature being widened and enriched by new developments, but they also deliberately stigmatize all other writing, to the extent that many people feel they have to be apologetic about anything they read that has not been officially approved of as 'serious' literature. The division creates a self-fulfilling prophecy and further divides both the literature and its readers into separate camps. (Though at night the dons sometimes go slumming and read great armfuls of detective stories and sometimes write them too.) To argue that 'literature' is actually an undifferentiated body of writing that has been published, is not to argue that it cannot be discussed, criticized, separated into genres, advocated or condemned, but the quite arbitrary division between 'popular' and 'serious' remains culturally quite unacceptable.

It has also been a tradition of the socialist movement in Britain that fictional and poetic writing have been important vehicles for the presentation of radical ideas. Mary Ashraf's excellent *Introduction to Working Class Literature in Great Britain*[18] details the whole history of the fictional promotion of challenging ideas from the Chartist novels of Ernest Jones, G.W.M Reynolds and Thomas Frost through the trade union novels of the 1870s and onwards up to Tressell's *The Ragged Trousered*

Philanthropists and the novels of Ethel Carnie prior to the General Strike of 1926. In the 1930s such writers as Howard Fast and Frank Tilsley managed to be both popular and political, but since the Second World War there has been little attempt by socialists to use fictional means to present oppositional ideas, though since the 1970s there have been many feminist novels which have created a flourishing fictional culture around the ideas and practices of the womens' liberation movement.[19]

It is important to recognize too that, contrary to many assumptions, working-class reading patterns have often been much more adventurous and internationalist than have patterns of middle-class reading. Engels noted this in the 19th century as we have seen, but it has also been true in this century. The great interest in the 1930s in American writing, and Russian literature too, was a feature of the reading habits of many working-class militants, as one understands both from the auto-biographies of that period and through interviews with members of that generation. In that same period though, the middle-class mass readership was reserved almost entirely for stolidly English country house detective novels and romances, in which the only foreigners were either spies, gigolos or mercenary Jews.[20]

Since the war the great popularity of such European writers as Camus, De Beauvoir, Sartre, Günther Grass and Heinrich Böll, of such American writers as Ray Bradbury, Richard Brautigan, Carson McCullers, Jack Kerouac, Norman Mailer, Henry Miller, William Burroughs, J.D. Salinger and Kurt Vonnegut Jnr., and for British writers such as Alexander Trocchi, Malcolm Lowry and Michael Moorcock, has been a feature, not of academic or bourgeois literary circles, but of the various phases of an oppositional youth culture that has had substantial working-class involvement. Even today working-class people with only secondary school education remain numerically the largest reading public in Britain, and still possibly the most eclectic and radical.[21]

Working Class Writing

One of the great difficulties in talking about the many diffuse and variegated traditions of working-class writing in Britain is the long shadow cast by Robert Tressell's extraordinary work *The Ragged Trousered Philanthropists*, first published in 1914 and still dominating many discussions about early socialist culture. For many working-class socialists it has attained an almost canonical status, to the extent that all other forms of fiction writing about class and politics are simply compared back to the Tressell novel and nearly always found wanting. During many years' involvement with socialist politics I have met a number of people for whom the problem of socialist culture would be solved by the arrival of an updated sequel to Tressell's book. Yet it is, of course, the mark of a major cultural achievement—and *The Ragged Trousered Philanthropists* is one—that it cannot be repeated, copied or simply modernized; its singularity is the measure of its achievement.

There was a very rich and complex culture of working-class writing in the 19th century, and even earlier, but since all of this work remains out of print any immediate project of reclaiming and re-evaluating a tradition remains impossible. (The only 20th-century collection of Chartist poetry was published in the Soviet Union after the war and has ironically become a collector's item in Britain. There continues to be much more serious work and interest in the literary achievements of the 19th-century British working class in the Soviet Union, the German Democratic Republic, and even the German Federal Republic, at an academic level, than in the country where these cultures were formed.) A difficulty in this century is that 'the miner's novel' has become, after Tressell's book, a secondary kind of archetypal proletarian fictional model, and other kinds of writing in other kinds in settings have tended to be overlooked. John Field's study of miners as novelists[21] details this important tradition up to 1939; in post-war working-class fiction the work of Len Doherty is again most well known, and that again explores the world of the mining community and its political culture. But in fact the 20th century has offered an enormous diversity of forms and settings including diaries (two recently published women's diaries, *Nella Last's War* and Diane Harpwood's fictionalized *Tea and Tranquillisers* are important and revealing testimonies for example), childhood evocations, prison literature, experimental novels, short stories, parodies, poems, craft autobiographies, the writings of worker-historians in the History Workshop movement: this is a many stranded and complex writing tradition. And though realism has been the major, though not the exclusive narrative mode, working-class realism has often been tempered by its own acerbic ironies, which have given this writing different levels of meaning in different circumstances and conditions of reading.

The more deeply you explore the many different forms of working-class writing in this century, the more problematic the concept of 'the working-class novel' or 'working-class literature' becomes. In my own reading, particularly of novels, quite radical misconceptions have had to be corrected. For what has become a kind of caricature setting for working class themes in bourgeois novels (Galsworthy's play *Strike* has much to answer for)—the factory gate, the lock-out and the work-force being starved back to work—hardly exists at all in workers' literature itself. The two major traumas that dominate the 20th century novel of working-class life are, not the strike, not the factory accident, but early and unwanted pregnancy and hasty marriage, or the back-street abortion. Homelessness and unemployment as other major themes compound and exacerbate the problems of the enforced and unhappy young marriage. A politics that addresses itself to people's felt difficulties, hopes and aspirations, actually needs to know what these are rather than assume them from some pre-conceived programme; working-class writing, in all its forms, provides an invaluable range of understanding of the dominant forms of oppression and division, and is therefore an integral and central part of an active and participatory working-class politics.

In fact it is becoming more and more clear that contemporary movements in adult literacy, people's history, and in the resurgence of working class writing through workshops and local publishing projects, have created a very active and new kind of oppositional cultural and educational politics involving increasingly large numbers of people. For whereas earlier working-class adult educational movements in Britain in this century, such as the National Council of Labour Colleges and the Workers' Educational Association, were strongly predicated on (and organized around) what it was assumed people *didn't know*, on their 'ignorance', these new forms of cultural struggle are based much more productively and radically on what people *do know*, and on the value and political significance of their experience and knowledge.[23] It is salutary to remember that it was the 'rediscovery' of adult illiteracy in Britain in the early 1970s that unleashed a tremendously liberating debate on the meaning of 'literacy', a debate which produced the argument that the ability to read was not enough and that opportunities for writing had to be included in any fully formed definition of cultural literacy. The reverberations of this debate extended as far as the universities, where English departments came under scrutiny for their preoccupation with criticism as the major mode of English studies, often completely excluding creative writing from any part of the English programme. The Ruskin College-inspired History Workshop movement, and more recently the network of working-class writers' workshops and local publishing projects affiliated to the Federation of Worker Writers and Community Publishers, have both been based on a generic commitment to people's own cultural productivity. It is interesting and significant that the ideology of such movements has found a ready acceptance in popular ideology, where a strong sense that history shouldn't just be 'about Kings and Queens' and also that 'all people have things worth saying' has produced a rare coincidence of radical practice with popular consciousness.

In what is often a very direct relationship between the writing produced by these movements and other kinds of political and cultural activity, they correspond to the kind of cultural process envisaged by Walter Benjamin in one of the opening pieces of his visionary text, *One-Way Street*:[24]

> Significant literary work can only come into being in a strict alternation between action and writing; it must nurture the inconspicuous forms that better fit its influence in active communities than does the pretentious, universal gesture of the book.

Popular literature

Radical or Marxist traditions of literary and cultural criticism have often been no more sympathetic to the cultural possibilities of popular literature in this country than have belles-lettristic, humanistic, scientific or Leavisite academic criticisms. Moralistic judgementalism is in fact generic to much radical cultural criticism. Yet surely a theory and practice of politics as a 'mass', or popular, activity ought to have an appropriate commitment to the creation and encouragment of a popular literature?

In staying so often so close to highly selective literary traditions, socialist criticism has also failed to understand and acknowledge the many new narrative developments and literary registers that popular genre fiction has in fact produced. This has been very obviously the case with the radical stylistic originality of American detective fiction, but it is also true of science fiction. An exception has been the recent essay by Peter Humm, 'Reading the lines: television and the new fiction' in *Re-Reading English*,[25] on the way in which popular American novelists like Kurt Vonnegut, Richard Brautigan and Robert Coover have emulated the discontinuous narrative forms of television to bring new life and a sense of modernity to popular writing, in a fiction that is also characterized by its social criticism and popular accessibility. These writers have in their texts broken down the strict literary divisions between fiction, autobiography and documentary writing by which traditional literary forms have actually divided people so frequently against their own experience, and these are very welcome and significant developments. It also has to be acknowledged that much popular literature is more international, global and totalizing, than much 'serious' national literature which is often very narrow in its range of geographical, historical and social settings. At one point in the 1960s it was reasonable to wonder whether any English novels were being written other than those set in North West London.

In the final analysis a materialist understanding of literature has to be based on an understanding of the economic and social relationships that inform and underpin the publishing industry. We can never know, in retrospect, what important writing in the past will never become available to us simply because it wasn't published. According to Escarpit 'historical selection' causes 80% of literary production to be forgotten within a year and 99% in twenty years.[26] Knowing that today publishers claim to receive about a hundred manuscripts for every novel they publish, it has to be realized that before the 'selective' tradition of literary criticism comes into play a radically more important process of selection has already taken place. Whilst publishing remains the plaything of market forces, there is no way in which we can have anything but a distorted and distorting sense of contemporary literature and writing. Current trends in fact suggest that quite soon the majority of books published might well be based, not on texts spontaneously written and submitted, but on work including novels, that publishers have commissioned people to write.[27] Thus capitalism doesn't simply distort the processes of cultural production but inverts them completely at its most intense and competitive level.

We need to argue for alternative forms of publishing outside the grip of market rationality, based on what a much larger number of people wish to write, and what others, including themselves, wish to read. Popular literature is not a generic kind of writing, it is about the size of readership.

Popular literature can, chameleon-like, change rapidly to reflect its environment. In the early 1970s the 'Literature Promotion Project' of the Swedish Social-Democratic government inaugurated a series of books by working-class writers that were published cheaply and sold on news-stands and in tobacco kiosks throughout Sweden.[28] In a matter of months these books became popular literature. Amongst young black people in Britain, poetry is popular literature today.

Publishing will have to become much more diverse and variegated if it is to reflect the many reading publics that actually exist at national, regional and local levels. We need more translations, but also more mother-tongue or bilingual publishing in Britain. Socialism has often been portrayed as a politics that seeks to conglomerate cultural and social choices, to regulate and dominate patterns of provision. We need to show, on the contrary, that a socialist cultural perspective opens up a whole range of new possibilities, actually works at many levels; is federal rather than centralizing and nationalist. 'Few but roses', urges traditional literary criticism. 'Let a hundred flowers bloom, let a hundred schools of thought contend,' we argue back.

Reading

2
The American Connection: The Masculine Style in Popular Fiction

But I do not regret my classical studies. I believe that the conventional defence of them is valid; that only by them can a boy fully understand that a sentence is a logical construction and that words have basic inalienable meanings, departure from which is either conscious metaphor or inexcusable vulgarity. Those who have not been so taught—most Americans and most women—unless they are guided by some rare genius, betray their deprivation.

Evelyn Waugh, *A Little Learning: An Autobiography*

The merits of American style are less numerous than its defects and annoyances, but they are more powerful. It is a fluid language, like Shakespearian English, and easily takes in new words, new meanings for old words, and borrows at will and at ease from the usages of other languages, for example the German free compounding of words and the use of noun or adjective as verb. Its overtones and undertones are not stylized into a social conventional kind of subtlety which is in effect a class language.

Final note—out of order. The tone quality of English speech is usually overlooked. This is infinitely variable, The American voice is flat, toneless and tiresome. The English tone quality makes a thinner vocabulary and a more formalized use of language capable of infinite meanings. Its tones of course are read into written speech by association. This makes good English a class language and that is its fatal defect. The English writer is a gentleman first and a writer second.

Raymond Chandler, *Notes on English and American Style*

> I read H.G. Wells, Arnold Bennett, all those people, but they weren't my kind of people. You always had the edge of class; and what intrigued me about the American writers—of course they had a class system as well—but they were talking the way we talked...What came through with the Americans was really a brutal and realistic attitude in language.
>
> Hemingway was the first because it was his idea that it was in the dialogue that you could do everything, rather than building up descriptive passages...The clarity of the phrase; he was using the vernacular which I liked.
>
> William Keal, retired trade-union and labour
> movement militant in personal interview

In recent years the growth of oral history projects in many countries testifies to the importance now given to popular experience, memory and activity recoverable through personal interviews. Many of these projects have concentrated on experiences of working life, family life, women's work and political activity, the struggle against fascism and the experience of war, trade-union and socialist politics, childhood recollections, and other kinds of direct, lived experience. Less attention has been paid to people's popular cultural experiences: the books they read, the films they saw, the music they listened to, the paintings and posters they remember, and the way in which these cultural-aesthetic experiences affected their lives. One's intuition has been that in earlier periods of working-class political activity, reading played an important part in widening people's understanding of the world, and poetry and fiction were often used as a form of moral confirmation that the world-view implied by socialist internationalism was one shared by many writers. In chapter 4 I examine the work of some British working-class writers in the 1930s who looked to aesthetic traditions—like expressionism—which were not to hand in British literary culture at the time.[1] In this essay I want to look at the way, in much the same period, that many working-class people in Britain, particularly those active on the left, looked to writers in other countries for forms of literature which addressed themselves more directly to the emotional and political experiences which their class position had brought to bear upon their lives.

The initial impulse for this essay arose out of a conversation some years ago with an elderly working-class political activist which has stayed in my mind, although the exact circumstances of the discussion have been forgotten. I had asked him about popular reading among his friends when he was younger, and he answered in words to the effect that: 'Of course, you must realize, a lot of men were very keen on American paper-backs—detective stories particularly; you wouldn't get them reading novels out of the library.' More recently I have made a point of asking about early reading patterns and preferences when interviewing older labour movement activists, and have had this assertion confirmed: that the interest in American writing of various kinds was significant and had important implications for the development of a popular vernacular style of writing in Britain. For instance, in an interview with Jack Dash, the retired rank-and-file dockers' leader, the first writer whom he mentioned as an important influence was Theodore Dreiser, the founding author of American naturalism. A list of other American writers quickly followed—John Dos Passos, James Farrell, Upton Sinclair; and this register of preferences has been repeatedly invoked, with additions, by other working-class readers and writers whom I have interviewed.

If the broader 'American connection' is obvious, in this chapter I want to concentrate on one particular genre within the body of twentieth-century American writing: the detective novel or 'thriller'. The study of this genre, it seems to me, most centrally raises the important question of a symbiotic link between genre writing and mainstream fiction in which, often, the genre writing is actually in the vanguard of exploring new narrative techniques, using vernacular styles of language democratically and unselfconsciously, and taking fiction into new geographical and social areas of life where the conventional novel is disinclined to venture. Moreover, against critics who wash their hands of popular literature,[2] I would cite the understanding of Gramsci, who insisted that one had to engage with and find a way of 'framing the question of what is called popular literature, that is of the success, among the masses of the people, of the *feuilleton* (adventure stories, thrillers, crime fiction, etc.), a success which owes a good deal too to the cinema and the newspapers. And it is this question which constitutes the greater part of the problem of the new literature as the expression of intellectual and moral renewal: for it is only among the readers of popular fiction that we shall find a sufficient and necessary public to create the cultural base for a new literature.'[3] And this is why the key role of American fiction in the development of British vernacular writing has to be understood, and why in particular it was within the genre of the American detective novel that certain writers were able to develop this popular form of literature into a sustained literary critique of urban capitalism, portraying human alienation in much more specific ways than conventional literature was at that point able to do.

The Detective Novel as Genre

The detective novel established itself from the First World War onwards as the most popular fictional form in European and American culture.[4] Significantly, historians of the genre, such as Julian Symons, point to William Godwin's *The Adventures of Caleb Williams or Things As They Are* as the first novel to use a murder as the central incident. As Godwin's sub-title indicates quite directly, the murder itself and its attendant ramifications were very much a device around which a political critique of prevailing economic and social relationships could be assembled. The false imprisonment of the main character is used by Godwin as the excuse for a lengthy and bitter attack on despotism, and reads even today as an admirable anarchist text. *Caleb Williams* was published just one year ofter the dangerously radical *Inquiry into the Principles of Political Justice* and might fairly, though not exclusively, be accounted for as expressing in fictional form some of Godwin's more direct political sentiments, as well as emotionally displacing genuine fears concerning his own personal safety, having sown the wind of political rights. The novel is also a story of arbitrary persecution and the adoption of a fugitive life, published in the decade which was to see the establishment of the first working-class political organization, the London Corresponding Society, and its rapid suppression.

Such radical origins were in the late nineteenth and early twentieth centuries partially displaced as the crime novel increasingly became a vehicle for the celebration of the property rights which wilful murder threatened to overturn or usurp. Thus in Godwin's novel the reader is made well aware that 'the law was better adapted for a weapon of tyranny in the hands of the rich, than for a shield to protect the humbler part of the community against their usurpations'. By the time of the era of the great gentlemen-detectives, however, the genre had become the perfect fictional form for the sacramentality of the executive institutions of the state. Audacious plots to steal the Crown Jewels, rob the Bank of England, poison cabinet ministers, counterfeit the legal tender of the realm, supplant false wills and thus break the ideological continuity of inheritance and primogeniture, issue false share certificates in a deliberate attempt to bankrupt the major companies; all these insidious projects were foiled by the superior minds of gentlemen close to the heart of the Establishment (meeting usually in one of the better London Clubs), whose principal task was to ensure the continuity and extension of the English ruling class, at home or abroad.

Yet even these novels could not but reveal (as do all genre discourses) some of the major ideological moods and apprehensions of their times. Walter Benjamin in *One-Way Street* thought that such novels in their descriptions of the ornate settings of the country houses and apartments, rich with tapestries, crowded with heavy dark wooden furniture, exotic ornaments and potted plants, revealed in a way other novels did not, 'part of the bourgeois pandemonium'.[5] Carlo Ginzburg more recently has outlined a detailed analogy between principles of crime detection as exemplified by Conan Doyle's Sherlock Holmes and the near contemporaneous principles of art detection as formulated by Giovanni Morelli and the observations of Freud in *The Psychopathology of Everyday Life*.[6] All three 'detectives' were developing theories based on the belief that it was in the seemingly insignificant gestures and details of human behaviour that the real clues to the personality were to be found.

The more exotic of the British novels of the period after Sherlock Holmes have been scrutinized by Claud Cockburn in his study, *Bestseller*.[7] Apart from a general glorification of British imperialism, many of these novels contained a strong vein of anti-Semitism, often linked with the menace of Bolshevism, together with a portrayal of the working class as an atavistic mob battering down the park railings. 'Consols are down to sixty-five!' is the newspaper headline which marks the full moment of horror in Guy Thorne's *When It Was Dark* (1903). Towards the end of Cockburn's period of study comes Warwick Deeping's immensely popular *Sorrel and Son*, a novel about middle-class failure partly compensated by the determination to hand something on and thus keep the continuity of inheritance intact: 'Sorrell found his poetry in figures. He was enjoying the romance of hard cash. These glittering sixpences, shillings, florins and half-crowns, they were the stars above his immediate world, and of far more significance and import than the stars. His means to an end, material plunder for immaterial needs. For with his savings he was going to arm his son against a world that babbled of socialism but still clutched a knife or a club...Only the indispensable and the individual few would be able to rise above the scramble of the industrial masses. It is the few who matter and who will always matter. So Sorrel thought.'[8]

In the 1920s and 1930s the crime novel dealt with many of the same fears as the earlier novels, but less exotically. The detective novel in this period was a form of fictional reassurance for a middle-class readership that the continuity of the class system was safe. Few detective novels in this period were based in urban settings, thus avoiding having to acknowledge the existence of an urban working class. Rather they were set, in the words of another critic of the genre, 'in a village, largely a commuters' village in the Home Counties where there's a church, a village inn, very handy for the odd Scotland Yard inspector and his man who come to stay for the regularly recurring crimes...'[9] Such working-class people who appeared in these novels did so as quasi-feudal retainers: cooks, butlers, domestic servants, gardeners and sometimes a local policeman who could exemplify the important class precept of 'rural idiocy'. George Orwell, writing his 'Bookshop Memories' in November 1936,[10] thought that the divide in popular fiction between 'the average novel—the ordinary, good-bad, Galsworthy-and-water stuff which is the norm of the English novel' and the detective novel was exclusively along gender lines: women reading the former and men the latter. This contrasts with the opinions of other commentators who have often assumed the readership of the country house murder to be mostly women. Uncharacteristically, Orwell failed to mention *class* tastes in this short impressionistic account of the reading public based on his own bookshop experience.

What is demonstrably true of the popular fiction of the 1930s, whether in the genres of romance, detective novel or exotic fantasy *(Blue Lagoon* or *Beau Geste)* is that working-class people were conspicuously absent among the characters. This was bound to cause considerable cultural tensions and pressures of non-recognition and marginality, even if these pressures were not articulated directly. Since it is clear to contemporary teachers of English in schools that working-class children always notice and register such massive facts of cultural invisibility in the fiction they read, there is no reason to suppose that working-class adults did not do so in earlier periods. Therefore it is not surprising that by the mid 1930s it was American writers who were beginning to find a wide readership in Britain, often among working-class men—a shift which by the late 1940s had become a very significant cultural fact.

In *The Uses of Literacy* (1957) Richard Hoggart was keenly aware of this turn towards a genre developed in another country with quite different social and cultural histories. Unfortunately he regarded the genre as an undifferentiated cultural commodity, read, he thought, for its sexual content above all, and, in only mentioning by name such writers as James M. Cain and Mickey Spillane, he failed to raise some of the more important questions concerning the attraction of the American detective novel for British readers. He was right to see that the prose style itself was something new—vernacular, terse, rather tough—though in describing it as 'debased Hemingway' he failed to consider that Hemingway's style itself had developed in a continuous relationship with the 'toughguy' school of thriller writing and could not be critically separated from it. Hoggart was also early in seeing the fact that because these novels were sited in the life of the 'megalopolis', they were attractive to the urban working class in Britain for whom the country-house murder was remote both in time and space.

It was immediately after the Second World War that American writing became firmly established in Britain. As John Sutherland noted: 'War stifled film-going and dining-out and had the paradoxical effect of stimulating reading while inhibiting the production of new books... People wanted fiction, and less was being produced. One consequence was the spectacular boom in American novels. Selling American rights was suddenly as easy as 'falling off a log', an agent, Juliet O'Hea, recalled.'[11] And it was in American fiction that many British working-class readers, including political militants, found a realism about city life, an acknowledgement of big business corruption, and an unpatronizing portrayal of working-class experience and speech which wasn't to be found in British popular fiction of the period, least of all in the crime novel obsessed as it was with the corpse in the library, the Colonel's shares on the stock market and thwarted passion on the Nile. Cultural mediation abhors a vacuum.

American Naturalism and the Vernacular Narrative

Of the many ways of understanding how literature 'reflects' the society in which it is produced, the study of genres is particularly useful in trying to understand the forms and meanings of popular literature. For the development of a genre is the development of a series of internal rules and understandings which make the structure of a cultural form at once familiar, recognizable and thus accessible. Developments in popular culture are necessarily developments within popular genres and forms. Russian formalist criticism in the writings of theorists like Shklovsky has argued that many important achievements in literature arise through 'the canonization of inferior (sub-literary) genres'; that Dostoevsky's novels were in essence crime novels, Pushkin's lyrics a refinement of 'album verses', and so on.[12] However, to write self-evidently within the popular forms of genre fiction is certainly to risk losing critical acceptance and approval, although the rewards of cultural influence are potentially much higher. This is why it has become a commonplace to credit Hemingway with the development of a terse, unrhetorical, unsentimental style of writing which gave such a fillip to the development of American vernacular writing, even though it is certainly possible that Hemingway actually took his lessons from the early short-story writing of dime magazine writer Dashiell Hammett. This is certainly the opinion of Julian Symons: 'People say sometimes that perhaps Hammett was influenced by Ernest Hemingway but in fact any influence there may have been was the other way round because Hammett had started writing his stories in the early 1920s: the first one appeared in 1921 well before Hemingway had started writing.'[13]

While such French writers as Camus and Sartre publicly admired the developments in technique which Hammett particularly brought to the novel in terms of its passionless, anonymous narrator and its milieu of cheap hotels, boarding houses, bars and cynical sexual alliances; orthodox literary opinion in Britain ignored the work of Hammett and other American detective novel writers as if it were beneath attention. It is salutary to remember Camus himself admitted that if it had not been for reading James M. Cain's *The Postman Always Rings Twice* he would not have had the idea and structure of psychological ambience with which to write *L'Etranger*, one of the most celebrated post-war European novels.[14] Other American writers in the detective genre were greatly admired in France. Horace McCoy, author of *They Shoot Horses, Don't They?* and *No Pockets in a Shroud* was described in the late 1930s as 'the most discussed American writer in France', admired for the 'objective lyricism' of his narrative style.[15]

British novelists, in contrast, have for the most part resisted the modernizing developments in narration and style developed in other countries and in genre writing, as if nothing had changed radically since Galsworthy. The insularity of much British fiction continues to be celebrated by its practitioners (although just in the past couple of years this seems finally to have been breached). Kingsley Amis's perorations sum up this attitude: 'I think that one of the reasons why, according to me, the English novel has got it over the American novel at the moment (sic) is because of things like English snobbery, and English conservatism and English class consciousness and all that kind of thing. Because I think that all this so-called wave of modernism has hit the English novel less hard than any other kind of novel. It seems to me that, little as I know of it, thank God, the French novel is in smithereens now, because of that wave.'[16] Making allowances for Amis's consistent liking for parody, there is a widely-held understanding represented in these remarks. Even when socialist writers in Britain have chosen to write within the framework of genre fiction—for example G.D.H. and Margaret Cole jointly wrote detective novels, as did C. Day Lewis and Christopher Caudwell among others—they failed to use the genre as a medium for any accompanying radical developments in technique or ideas, but rather let the genre determine the form and content of their novels almost completely. It is no wonder that many working-class readers, particularly men, found American writing so much more accessible in style and subject matter in comparison to the classical formalism of the English novel of suburban manners—and murders.

The great popular early masterpiece of American naturalism was Theodore Dreiser's *An American Tragedy*, published in 1925. Dreiser himself had been brought up in bitter poverty in one of the mill-towns of Indiana and became a journalist on leaving school. That many important American writers started out as journalists—Dreiser, Hemingway, Chandler—shows a significantly different cultural and class route to writing than that of the majority of English writers of the same period who were likely to be public school graduates with some form of private income and connections with the major publishing houses. Dreiser's writing was immensely detailed in its descriptions of place and circumstance: H.L. Mencken wrote in an introduction to one edition of *The American Tragedy* that if a train time-table was given in a Dreiser novel it was guaranteed to be right, and that every street scene in every novel had its exact original in some American town or city. Dreiser's sympathies were with the American common people, despite their faults, and he wrote about them unpatronizingly and with considerable insight. It is actually impossible to imagine a work of popular fiction published in Britain at this time (1925) in which working-class people could be portrayed realistically and sympathetically.

Dreiser's novel was based on a real murder case in 1906 in which a young man drowned his pregnant girlfriend and was executed for his crime. In Dreiser's version, the young man plans such a murder, but when the time comes to carry this out cannot go through with it. However, by accident the girl does drown and because of a mass of circumstantial evidence as to the young man's intentions he is tried for murder, found guilty and executed. This device was also adopted by James M. Cain in *The Postman Always Rings Twice*, wherein someone is condemned for the intention rather than the act. This was the irony much admired by Camus. Thus the plot could hardly be more simple; the power and interest lay in the way in which it described the lives and values of American urban life, the ambitions and corruptions, the dreams of success set against the miseries of slums and the prisons.

By the time *An American Tragedy* was published, both Hammett and Hemingway had short stories published. Hammett had his first work in print in 1921, and Hemingway's small collection of 'fragments', *In Our Time*, came out in 1923. All argument about who actually influenced whom must remain, unfortunately, speculation; however the connection between the two is not in doubt. Both had been trained in writing through their work: in Hemingway's case as a reporter and in Hammett's as a Pinkerton detective. Hemingway acknowledged the influence of the style-sheets of the *Kansas City Star* with their instructions to 'avoid the use of adjectives, especially such extravagant ones as *splendid, gorgeous, grand, magnificent*'. ('The best rules I ever learned for the business of writing' recalled Hemingway.) There was also the discipline involved in transmitting stories by transatlantic cable which put an economic premium on each word. Hammett's early writing had consisted of case reports about his work at the detective agency which in later life Hammett recalled for their 'literary quality.' As has been noted, Julian Symons, in his history of the genre, thought Hammett was the initiating writer in the development of the austere vernacular narrative so much admired in Hemingway. André Malraux thought the same, commenting in 1937 that Hammett was the 'technical link' between Dreiser and Hemingway.[17] This question is so important because it is usually considered that Hemingway's austere, objective style can be attributed in part to the influence of Pound and Gertrude Stein in Paris, whereas it may well be that his style owed as much, if not more, to the developments achieved by Dashiell Hammett in his dime magazine stories: a rather less exotic parentage but one which at least acknowledges the modernizing pressure of popular, vernacular taste.

There were more direct material pressures which also helped to produce this condensed style of writing. Of the twenty-five stories Hammett had published between November 1922 and June 1924, half were less than 2,500 words. Hemingway's first collection, *In Our Time*, is simply a collection of short sketches, some less than one hundred words in length.

Neither Hammett nor Hemingway began by regarding themselves as apprentice novelists, but rather as people who wanted to use writing as sharply and clearly as possible to describe an incident, recreate a conversation, portray violence and fear in a few short sentences. Both cultivated a prose style that had the appearance of objective reporting. As Hemingway said about his own writing: 'The test of a book is how much good stuff you can throw away. I use the oldest words in the English language when I write. People think I'm an ignoramus who doesn't know the ten-dollar words. I know the ten-dollar words. But there are older, better words....'[18] Hammett narrated nearly all his short stories and early novels between 1923 and 1930 in the words of his anonymous private investigator working for the Continental Detective Agency, using the vocabulary of such a man rather than the vocabulary and syntax of an omniscient narrator. Chandler, when writing about the importance of Hammett in establishing the genre of the 'hard-boiled' American detective novel, pointed out how Hammett's radical literary break-through arose out of his exactness of ear for popular speech: 'He had a literary style, but his audience didn't know it, because it was in a language not supposed to be capable of such refinements. They thought they were getting a good meaty melodrama written in the kind of lingo they imagined they spoke themselves. It was, in a sense, but it was much more. All language begins with speech, and the speech of common men at that, but when it develops to the point of becoming a literary medium it only looks like speech.' And with the extensive use of the vernacular, particularly in Hemingway's second collection, significantly titled *Men Without Women* (1927), came the now familiar 'Hemingway' narrative syntax built up with short, lapidary sentences.

The Emergence of a 'Masculine' Style

From the beginning this new development in narrative style was always described in terms associated with masculinity, in the critical reception of both writers. Of *The Maltese Falcon*, one reviewer thought Hammett's writing 'better than Hemingway; since it conceals not softness but hardness'. Another reviewer of the same novel referred to 'the sheer force of Hammett's hard, brittle writing (which) lifts the book out of the general run of crime spasms and places it aloof and alone as a brave chronicle of a hard-boiled man, unscrupulous, conscienceless, unique.' The prose of Hemingway's first collection, *In Our Time*, is described as being made up of 'stubby verbal forms speeded in instances up to the brute, rapid, joyous jab of blunt period upon period. Hemingway's vocabulary is largely monosyllabic, and mechanical and concrete...Hemingway's style...in its very experimental stage shows the outline of a new, tough, severe and satisfying beauty related equally to the world of machines and the austerity of the red man.'[20] The subsequent collection was reviewed by Cyril Connolly in the *New Statesman* thus: *'Men Without Women* is a collection of grim little stories told in admirable colloquial dialogue with no point, no moral and no ornamentation. They are about bull-fighters, crooks, crook prize-fighters, crook peasants, dope fiends and soldiers in hospital. The title is intended to strike the note of ferocious virility which characterizes the book, which is, however, by no means free from the strong silent sentimentality latent in this attitude.'[21]

The understanding that there are 'masculine' and 'feminine' literary styles is not new, though it probably doesn't really surface as an explicit form of criticism until after the First World War and the break-up of traditional narrative forms under the impact of modernism. It has to be remembered that English Literature as a university subject itself was considered a 'feminine' subject until the appearance of 'scientific' (i.e. masculine) linguistic criticism, developed by I.A. Richards in the 1920s, and that historically the novel was the one cultural form, in the nineteenth century particularly, in which women earned for themselves an equal, if not superior, status to that of men. Thus a noted 'authority' on style in this period, Sir Arthur Quiller-Couch, could point out some of the gender rules for writing: 'Generally use transitive verbs, that strike their objects and use them in the active voice, eschewing the stationary passive, with its little auxiliary is's and was's, and its participles getting in the light of your adjectives, which should be few. For, as a rough law, by his use of the straight verb and by economy of adjectives, you can tell a man's style, if it be masculine or neuter, writing or composition.'[22]

The narrative styles of Hemingway and Hammett are clear examples of this renunciation of all detail other than the action, the dialogue and a minimal description of the setting. No characters ever have their thoughts articulated; what we know about their inner lives has to be inferred from their speech and their behaviour. The omnipotent, all-seeing narrator of conventional narrative discourse has been dispensed with, and one can argue that the 'dime novel' arrived at this position several decades ahead of the 'nouveau roman'.

In between the first edition of one of the episodes from *In Our Time* and the revised edition published eight years later, 'Hemingway reduced the 241 words to 121, the more than thirty descriptive adjectives to ten, shortened the length of the sentences, changed some of the adjectives to past participles, added several present participles, and made all the sentences simple and declarative.'[23] Nothing remotely similar to this modernizing, democratizing process was happening at this time in the English narrative style. This is why when Chandler (who had been educated in England at Dulwich College) started to write, following in the style of Hammett, he stated that, 'I had to learn American just like a foreign language...Thank heaven that when I tried to write fiction I had the sense to do it in a language that was not all steamed up with rhetoric.'[24]

This concern with objectifying the language of the novel was one which accounted for the French enthusiasm for the 'hard-boiled' American detective novel, an appreciation of style which was part of a reciprocal admiration between French and American literature. It was, after all, one of the most famous maxims of Voltaire that 'the adjective is the enemy of the verb'. Flaubert's perfectionism was the standard by which a number of American writers at this time judged themselves. In Hemingway's *Green Hills of Africa* the narrator tells Kandinsky that one of the most important things for a writer to have is 'the discipline of Flaubert'. In writing to his publisher, Hamish Hamilton, in 1949, Chandler listed the eight stories in European literature he most admired as 'all perfect': three were by Flaubert.

Both Hemingway and Chandler thought American English to be much more open to modern experience than the formalism of the language they found among the English upper class they met in London or in Paris. One of Hemingway's first published miniatures for *In Our Time* was a parody of an English officer's speech: 'It was a frightfully hot day. We'd jammed an absolutely perfect barricade across the bridge. It was simply priceless....' In a number of his novels, characters are often to be found commenting sarcastically on formal English speech. In *The Sun Also Rises*, Jake Barnes remarks that 'When you are with the English, you get into the habit of using English expressions in your thinking. The English spoken language, the upper classes', anyway, must have fewer words than the Eskimo.' In Chandler's essay comparing the two styles of language, he thought American English, '...emotional and sensational rather than intellectual. It expresses things experienced rather than ideas...Why then can it produce great writing or at any rate writing as great as this age is likely to produce? The answer is, all the best American writing has been done by men who are, or at some time were, cosmopolitans. They found here a certain freedom of expression, a certain richness of vocabulary, a certain wideness of interest...compared with it at its best, English has reached the Alexandrian stage of formalism and decay.'[25]

One or two radical critics in England at this time recognized the problem of the opaqueness and self-aggrandizement of English narrative style. In 1931 the English poet and art critic (and philosophical anarchist) Herbert Read published his detailed analysis of *English Prose Style*. In separating out the various structural and linguistic elements which combine to form what we call 'prose style', he pointed to a proper interest in narrative as being the most distinctive weakness of English writing: 'good narrative writing is comparatively rare in English literature. There is a human failing which urges us to elaborate and decorate our descriptions; it is perhaps merely the desire to infuse an objective activity with something of the personality of the narrator.'[26]

Although there is a tradition of narrative simplicity in English fiction, a speed and economy in relating a story, such as is found in Defoe, Bunyan and in the tradition of the picaresque novel, there is a rather stronger tradition which has been favoured in which the novel has become a rhetorical form, in which detailed description of place, custom and dress, together with an appropriate amount of moral reflection, tend to weigh down the progress of the narrative to a debilitating degree. The enormous effort—articulated most explicitly by Matthew Arnold—to make English literature a substitute for religion, the moral currency of the culture, may have given the novel a greater sense of its own importance, but this has often been achieved at the expense of its story-telling, vernacular, democratic obligations. As Read himself noted of the pre-novel literary forms: 'In the older forms of narrative, such as the Fable, the Allegory, and the Parable, the action is coherent and unimpeded.'[27] The novel, though, in its development within English culture, has often almost tried to dispense with action altogether. This does go some way towards explaining that massive disjunction in this century between the novel of manners and the popular novel of action and narrative speed.

The Influence of Hammett and Hemingway

Between them, then, Hammett and Hemingway developed a tough, masculine, vernacular (or demotic) style of writing which helped transform and democratize American literature from the 1930s onwards, and which provided a vicarious excitement and a sense of freedom for a number of British readers, for whom the English short story and novel were still preoccupied with provincial manners. Hammett and Hemingway evoked a harsh (but definitely twentieth-century) world of mining towns, transit camps, life on the road, seedy bars, boxing rings, corrupt city governments, and a proletarian politics that took guns and baseball bats to picket lines. At the centre of these stories were the stoical men who recorded everything they saw, who tried to retain some basic decency, tried to put things straight and restore a sense of order: Hemingway's Nick Adams; Hammett's anonymous agency detective who finally, in *The Maltese Falcon*, becomes the mythical Sam Spade. Such characters were quintessentially the 'degraded' heroes (Barthes) engaged in a 'demoniacal' (Lukács) search for authentic values of the twentieth-century European novel, but they achieved a reading public far beyond that of the 'literary' novel.

In Hammett's hands, especially, the detective novel became an important vehicle for radical social criticism, without reading like a polemical text. The assumption which informs all Hammett's work is that the police, politicians and big business combine together to run the city administration in their own interests, even though this often involves murder, gang-slayings, bribery and perjury. The scale of civic corruption in *Red Harvest* and *The Glass Key* is extraordinary, yet it is cleverly treated as a back-cloth, or night-town milieu, in which the detective works in response to other interests. The jungle of the cities which Brecht wanted to portray to European theatre audiences, Hammett had already fictionalized for his dime magazine readers. Brecht's 'City of Mahagonny' (1929) is directely related to Hammett's 'Poisonville' in *The Red Harvest* of the same year, sharing a common setting, imagery and *dramatis personae*. Wim Wenders's film *Hammett* (1982) acknowledges that shared understanding in the expressionist garishness of his settings of Chinatown and the waterfront, quite deliberately non-naturalistic, and also in the way that by setting the film entirely at night, except for brief opening and closing sequences in daylight showing us the apartment block in which Hammett is writing, the film suggests that we are spending an evening in the theatre.

Yet as well as economic and political corruption, which are conventions of the 'hard-boiled' school of writing, there is also the convention of sexual corruption in which women belong to the forces of evil. For women always play an obstructive role in such fiction, threatening to emasculate or betray the stoical heroes on their lonely journeys through the mean streets or on the adolescent camping expeditions, or during the final shoot-out which brings the typical detective novel to its end. Women do not figure as significant characters or strong characters in Hemingway's work: the early Nick Adams stories are about the painful decision to break off the relationship with Marjorie and its choice of a single life of action and self-discovery. In *A Farewell to Arms*, Hemingway's contribution to the great love novel, the woman dies on the last page leaving the man to walk off into the night, on his own, in the rain. In the detective novels of Hammett and Chandler this ending is developed into an established convention of the genre. In Hammett's *Red Harvest* the principal woman character and potential lover of the detective is murdered two-thirds of the way through the book; in *The Dain Curse* the central female figure is saved from heroin addiction by the detective, but when she makes a sexual advance towards him is rejected; in *The Maltese Falcon* the same *femme fatale* is handed over to the police at the end, even though Sam Spade loves her; and in *The Glass Key* the detective does leave at the end with a woman to travel to another city, but it is an arrangement of convenience and made without any emotional commitment.

In Chandler's novels the misogyny becomes more extreme. One recent and convincing Chandler critic, Michael Mason,[28] points to the increasingly obvious development in the novels of Marlowe's own homosexual sentiments, which are made more pronounced by the increasing dislike of women evident in the writing. The 'tough guy' novel is, in fact, predicated on a deep ambiguity about sexual identity. In a collection of 'Casual Notes on the Mystery Novel' (1949) Chandler seemed to be rationalizing a state of affairs with regard to his own detective creation, Marlowe, when he renounced the possibility of any kind of achieved and settled sexual relationship for the detective in the mystery novel: 'The only effective kind of love interest is that which creates a personal hazard for the detective—but which, at the same time, you instinctively feel to be a mere episode. A really good detective never gets married.'[29]

Chandler's own writing, based as it was originally on a total admiration for the styles of Hammett and Hemingway, often specifically mentioned, became increasingly sophisticated and moved away from the popular and demotic. The descriptions of the settings became longer, although they were always characterized by a mordant and acerbic irony. The similes piled on top of each other, the dialogue became more consciously dry-witted and more often self-consciously studded with intellectual and literary allusions, the perorations on human weakness, civic corruption and sexual infidelity became longer. The cost of refining the genre was that it began to look towards a different readership for approval as it became more self-consciously literary and settled back again into conventional narrative forms. The one thing that Chandler continued to share with the earlier 'tough-guy' writers was a real hatred of police corruption and police brutality. In his last complete novel, *The Long Goodbye*, his portrait of the police is quite savage and bitter. The one honest police officer in the novel is described by Marlowe as talking 'like a Red'. 'I wouldn't know' the officer replies, 'I ain't been investigated yet.' This was written in the early period of McCarthyism. Elsewhere in the novel a character tells Marlowe, 'That's the difference between crime and business. For business you gotta have capital. Sometimes I think it's the only difference.'

It was for such insights that the 'tough-guy' novel came under rearguard attack from one of America's most distinguished establishment critics, Jacques Barzun, who defended the 'ethical, civilized, and in the best sense literary' qualities of the classic detective genre, against the 'pseudo-realism' and 'nihilistic vandalism' of Hammett and Chandler, noting, with not a little dash of red-baiting, that 'the tough story was born in the Thirties and shows the Marxist colouring of its birth years.'[30] Condemned by the literary establishment in America for its sordid milieux and the cynical (but dangerously radical) eye cast on the existence of massive civic corruption, it was also denounced by Communist aestheticians in the same period. Many derogatory references were made to the detective novel during the course of the Soviet Writers' Congress of 1934, of which Zhdanov's was most scathing: 'The "illustrious persons" of bourgeois literature—of that bourgeois literature which has sold its pen to capital—are now thieves, police sleuths, prostitutes, hooligans.'[31]

There is no sense here of an understanding that to write about the underworld, to portray life in the jungle of the cities, was in many ways to be writing about a milieu that most directly represented the ferocious struggles of capital and its political wings in Europe and America in the 1920s and 1930s. Professional literary criticism may not have realized this, but for a very large reading public the American thriller confirmed that big business and corrupt politicians combined between them to run the major cities of Europe and America, and could often count on a compliant police force to facilitate and consolidate the tyrannies of these wholly corrupt and ruthless alliances.

Chandler's influence on the British reading public was in one instance more direct than simply being a writer whose books were avidly read; as he often complained his work enjoyed a more enthusiastic reception in Britain than in America. A year before his death, while staying in London, he read an extract of an autobiographical novel by Frank Norman in *Encounter* magazine. Frank Norman was an orphan brought up in a Dr Barnardo's Home and sent to prison at an early age on a robbery charge. His prison memoirs, *Bang to Rights*, published in 1958, were an important contribution to the new wave of working-class realism which broke across British culture in the late 1950s and early 1960s. Having read the *Encounter* extract, Chandler offered to write a foreword: 'There is no damned literary nonsense about his writing. Frank Norman writes swiftly and closely about things...An observation so sharp should not be lost to the world. We need it. He has it.'[32]

In the same year, Brendan Behan's *Borstal Boy* was published, as was Alan Sillitoe's *Saturday Night and Sunday Morning*. Neither Behan, Sillitoe, Bernard Kops, Bill Naughton and the other vernacular writers who emerged in that period chose to write genre fiction; they wrote prison autobiographies, childhood autobiographies (to which Keith Waterhouse and Leslie Thomas contributed two fine books), or short stories and novels based on modern working-class picaresque heroes: Sillitoe's Arthur Seaton, Bill Naughton's Alfie. Yet the great narrative and stylistic caesura which separates their writing from that of popular socialist novelists of the pre-war period, such writers as Howard Fast and Frank Tilsley, for example, could not have been resolved in British writing without the direct influence of the American realist and vernacular tradition. For by the 1940s and 1950s, other American writers like Steinbeck and Salinger were being avidly read in Britain, and their crisp, popular colloquial style was widely admired and emulated.

In Britain the most radical attempt to use the detective genre as a way of writing about class and city life from a socialist critical perspective has been William McIlvanney's *Laidlaw* published in 1977. Laidlaw is a disillusioned detective in Glasgow working on a very unpleasant rape and murder of a young girl on her way home from a discotheque. As a portrait of working-class Glasgow, of the Protestant/Catholic divide, of the deep and self-destructive entrenchments of attitudes about gender roles, and of the Byzantine moral world of an urban police force, it is extraordinarily good. Although much better than anything Amis, Braine or Wain have written in the 1970s, their novels gather immediate status as serious contemporary fiction, whilst McIlvanney's is condemned to the second division of genre fiction, even though it won the 'Crime Writers' Association Silver Dagger Award' (sic).

What continues to be obvious, it seems, is that the 'tough-guy' vernacular style of writing, is very much the narrative style which many working-class *male* writers adopt as the appropriate register and syntax for writing about contemporary class experience. The settings are often ones detached from routine daily life (including the workplace) and are often exclusively male: betting shops, pubs, cafes. Family life is not dealt with in great detail. From Sillitoe's quick-tongued, articulate, go-down-fighting, working-class rebels, via Bill Naughton's eponymous Alfie and Alan Bleasedale's Franny Scully, the narrative ideology is one of continuity with that developed through the connection with American vernacular realism. No one can doubt the strengths of this narrative style—its celebration of individual resistance to arbitrary authority, its quickwitted repartee in response to authoritarianism, the emphasis on the moral autonomy of the narrator or main character; yet there are disadvantages. The most obvious is the avoidance of engaging with the reality of personal and sexual relationships, or, when tackled, denying the mutuality and reciprocity of such relationships. The ideological roots of this persona combine a mixture of Protestant individualism with a dash of iron-in-the-soul existentialism. Its material basis is to be found in the relative autonomy which men possess within the culture of work and social relationships compared with women. The world in which the vernacular flourishes is that city life in which the semi-independent, entrepreneurial working class is to be found: in the street markets, among cab drivers, self-employed tradesmen, and of course among those involved in crime.

It is not surprising, therefore, that many women, including working-class women, feel estranged from popular vernacular writing, perhaps because it clearly emanates from a world from which they have been historically and culturally excluded. They feel, no doubt correctly, that it reflects a certain kind of working-class male bravura which, by definition, is oppressive. Yet, while accepting the weight of these criticisms, it is still important to defend, critically, vernacular realism because of its narrative strength and popular accessibility to the language of everyday life. Can a vernacular style of writing be developed which is not gender-specific and oppressive? (One still cannot imagine a woman writing, 'Down these mean streets a woman must go, a woman who is herself not mean....')

The question is probably a decisive one. Economic and cultural oppression have historically reduced and limited the narrative styles (among many other cultural modes) by which that oppression can be resisted and overthrown. Despite the development of many new forms of cultural production since the 1930s, the production of popular literature remains the site of very serious cultural struggles which need to be addressed more consciously than they have been so far by socialists.

3

The Popular Literature
of the Second World War

It is commonly claimed that the Second World War, unlike the First, produced no significant body of literature in English. The poetry of Julian Grenfell, Rupert Brooke, Edward Thomas, Isaac Rosenberg, Wilfrid Owen and Sigfried Sassoon, together with such important autobiographical works as Edmund Blunden's *Undertones of War*, Robert Graves's *Goodbye To All That* and Vera Brittain's *Testament of Experience*, are cited as composing a profound range of imaginative writing that embodied the terrible loss and enormity of 'The Great War'. Very little work of the same intensity, it has been argued, emerged from the Second World War, though the achievements of Sidney Keyes, Alun Lewis, Keith Douglas, Hamish Henderson and Henry Reed in poetry are mentioned as constituting a small qualification that prevents the complete dismissal of the literature of the 1939-1945 period.

Within the limits of what is defined as literature by the 'selective tradition', this may well be true. In a selection of general critical works about the literature of this period, such as *The Penguin Guide to English Literature: The Modern Age* (1961),[1] Robert Hewison's *Under Siege* (1979),[2] Walter Allen's *Tradition and Dream* (1964)[3] and Ronald Blythe's anthology *Components of the Scene* (1966),[4] such definitions are uncritically employed. Thus an enormous body of writing about the Second World War, such as that contained in the widely-read literature of escape stories, concentration camp memoirs, resistance novels and autobiographies of combatants, is passed over in complete silence. This is particularly noticeable in Blythe's anthology which is subtitled 'An anthology of the *prose* and poetry of the Second World War' (my italics), which contains not one piece of documentary writing, includes not one account of prison camp or concentration camp life, nor any form of writing by or about life in 'the other ranks'. The cultural myopia of English literary criticism could not be more evident. The great stone wall—or barbed wire fence in this case—which separates 'Literature' from 'writing', then as now, cuts a swathe through any possibility of a common discourse of writing and creates many more cultural blockages and difficulties than it solves.

For the flow between the genres and achievements of popular literature and that of the 'selective tradition' has been historically continuous and reciprocal, and the denial of this fact continues to be at the heart of the popular alienation from literature, and the elitism of academic English studies. The 'selective tradition' makes critical life easier at an academic level, for there are certainly many less books to read, silences to register, narrative forms to acknowledge and genres to accommodate. But critical work ought not to be easy, because what is at stake is not the dismissal or celebration of discrete works, single novels, or individual poems. Rather it is whole literatures and cultural processes, social relationships of reading, writing and publishing, which, if acknowledged and supported, could work for the wider processes of humanism and cultural self-activity, but, if dismissed, could leave the social activities of reading and writing (that is to say, literature) ineluctably at the whim of market forces. Popular literature—and popular culture—needs more critical attention and commitment then the 'selective tradition', not less.

It is likely that in the 1950s the most widely read books in Britain were books that dealt with the experiences of male combatants in the Second World War, a cultural phenomenon which literary histories have hardly acknowledged. The only qualification on this literature's status as *the* popular literature of that decade is that its readership was almost exclusively male. Women's experiences of the impact of the Second World War were largely ignored, except for translations of a small number of accounts by women of involvement in European resistance movements or as survivors of the Nazi concentration camps. The most notable of these were *The Dairy of Anne Frank*, Micheline Maurel's *Ravensbruck* and Anne-Marie Walters's *Moondrop to Gascony*, all of which were published in paperback in Britain in the 1950s.

In total we are talking about not many more than twenty paperback books, all published in the 1950s, yet between them they were sold in millions and read in even larger numbers. As a secondary school student in this period I would have to say that they were the staple reading diet of myself and all my school peers, and the sales figures also suggest that they were the staple reading diet of the adult male British reading public, and, possibly, of a significant proportion of the female reading public. What follows is fairly comprehensive list of titles, publication dates and number of editions:

The Wooden Horse, Eric Williams, 1949 (9 editions by 1965)
The Dam Busters, Paul Brickhill, 1951 (21 editions by 1968)
The Bridge over the River Kwai, Pierre Boulle, 1952 (17 editions by 1968)
The Colditz Story, P.R.Reid, 1952 (14 editions by 1974)
The White Rabbit, Bruce Marshall, 1952 (4 editions by 1954)
Two Eggs on My Plate, Oluf Reef Olsen, 1952 (3 editions by 1955)
The Naked Island, Russell Braddon, 1952
Boldness Be My Friend, Richard Pape, 1953 (6 editions by 1972)
Scourge of the Swastika, Lord Russell of Liverpool, 1954 (16 editions by 1976)
Bomber Pilot, Leonard Cheshire, 1954 (298,000 undated)
House of Dolls, Ka-Tzetnik 135633, 1956 (10 editions by 1958)
Camp on Blood Island, J.M. White & V. Guest, 1958 (6 editions in 1958)
Moondrop to Gascony, Anne-Marie Walters, 1946 (paperback edition 1951)
Cockshell Heroes, C.E. Lucas Phillips, 1956
Ravensbruck, Micheline Maurel, 1959
Knights of the Bushido, Lord Russell of Liverpool
Ill Met By Moonlight, W.Stanley Moss, (1956)
The Great Escape, Paul Brickhill, 1951
The Diary of Anne Frank, 1953, (45 editions by 1981)

(This list is by no means definitive, and details as to publishing history are those contained in the copies I have collected over the years. Some of these books have continued to be reprinted. I have listed only paperback titles.)

There were, of course, many other books written about the war which were not, significantly, taken up by the paperback publishers and promoted as those above were. Some of these books expressed a class position and a politics distinct from what was generally published and promoted, and included what were probably two of the finest novels about the experiences of combatants of the Second World War: Alexander Baron's *From the City, From the Plough* (1948) and Dan Billany's *The Trap* (1950), both written by working-class socialists. Theirs was a view that was at odds with the way in which a popular cultural history of the war was being reconstructed in popular literature during the era of the Cold War—they remained in hardback and thus did not receive widespread circulation. Stuart Hood's *Pebbles From My Skull* (1963), which was also oppositional in its sensibility and politics, was published at a much later date than the majority of war-time accounts and thus entered 'literature' in a different guise and through a different door. Too late to intervene and disturb the consensus of popular war literature in the 1950s, it nevertheless helped to inspire the wave of popular autobiographical writing in Britain during the 1970s generated by the oppositional culture of local publishing, and its final paragraph became one of the most widely quoted epigrams of that new literature:

> We may record the past for various reasons: because we find it interesting; because by setting it down we can deal with it more easily; because we wish to escape from the prison where we face our individual problems, wrestle with our particular temptations, triumph in solitude and in solitude accept defeat and death. Autobiography is an attempted jail-break. The reader tunnels through the same dark.[5]

Thus the role of publishing is, and historically always has been, crucial to the framing and construction of popular memory and popular consciousness. Certainly in the literature of the Second World War, such key books as those above, significantly never received the promotion that others embodying more acceptable political and class values did.

The popular literature of the Second World War can be fairly clearly divided into four distinct genres: escape stories, heroism in war, stories of resistance, and testimonies of German and Japanese war crimes. Each genre had its distinctive traits and conventions; each genre has over time developed successors in popular literature and new forms of development, a not unsurprising occurrence since popular literature, like all other forms of popular culture, is a historical phenomenon and proceeds by adaptation and development. Thus escape stories flowed back into the consistently popular genre of prison literature; the tales of heroism developed into the male adventure novels of such writers as Alistair MacLean and Jack Higgins; the resistance novels formed part of the literary culture of post-war existentialism; and the literature of the war crimes was superseded by the Nazi war novels of such writers as Sven Hassel, H.H. Kirst and the fictional Nazi nightmares described by John Sutherland in his chapter on war literature in *Bestsellers: Popular fiction of the 1970s.* A swastika on a book-cover remains a powerful sales strategy, through some strange atavism.

Escape Stories

Escape stories of the First and Second World Wars are exceptional within the wider genre of prison literature in that they deal, unusually, with the experiences of the middle and upper classes under prison conditions. There is not one account of escape from either war written (or rather published) by a rank and file member of the Services, though clearly such men made escape attempts and no doubt some succeeded. The first of the escape accounts, and probably the best, was Eric Williams's *The Wooden Horse*, first published in 1949. The story of the escape is well known: Williams and two other officers dug a tunnel out of the prison camp they were in and disguised their activities by digging each day from under a wooden vaulting horse placed near the fence and used for exercise by other prisoners who were party to the plan. The escape was successful and using forged passes, Williams and one of the other escapers managed to travel to a seaport on the Baltic and escape to Denmark, and later to England, with the help of members of the Danish resistance and some French Communist workers billeted in Germany.

Williams's account of the routines of prison life remains the most detailed and convincing of all these books in that he spent time portraying other characters and the effect of imprisonment on them, and acknowledged without sarcasm the occasionally beneficial effects on himself and his fellow prisoners of such virtues as domestication and mutual support. His portrayal of a hut-mate, David, who retreated into a fantasy world of running a farm in his own imagination, is both moving and convincing writing. Other writers in the genre never even saw imprisonment as a particular social condition, with a history and a psychology, and describe prison life as little different from dormitory life at public school. Much the most frightening part of *The Wooden Horse* is the part dealing with their journey through Germany to the Baltic and their days of waiting to make contact with a boat that would smuggle them out. For during this time they had to pretend to be foreign workers with authorized travel permits and risked being caught, and possibly shot, every hour of the day. Williams is honest enough to admit that for much of the time when they were on the run he would rather have been back in the prison camp, so great was the fear and nightmare of discovery. After the war Williams went on to become a writer and the biographical note that prefaces the paperback edition of *The Wooden Horse* shows exactly how these escape accounts were framed in a context of rugged individualism and led on to the popular literature of male adventure:

> He now travels the world, by Land Rover and a small boat, and writes adventure novels which continue the theme of his escape books—man alone, struggling to preserve his freedom and integrity in spite of the odds against him.

P.R. Reid's *Colditz Story*, first published in 1952, remains in print and has also been filmed and made into a popular television series in the 1970s. Even more than Williams's publisher, Reid introduces his account in terms of war and imprisonment as a backcloth for the more important values of individualism and masculinity:

> The inspiration of escape books lives in men's memories and serves to keep alive the spirit of adventure.
> I can think of no other sport that is the peer of escape, where freedom, life, and loved ones are the prize of victory, and death the possible though by no means inevitable price of failure.

Such books as these have been quite crucial in post-war Britain in giving a context to a notion of 'freedom' that is totally abstract and talismanic, but which has continued to exert a powerful influence in the vocabulary of conservatism as a rallying call against collectivist, communitarian and many other kinds of mutual association. That for Reid a notion of freedom takes priority over 'life', or 'loved ones', exemplifies the power of this abstraction. Clearly as a felt value in a prison camp during a war whose outcome was uncertain such a value was understandable; but in peacetime it was still used as a moral currency which had no reference whatsoever to material conditions and relationships.

What is particularly ironic about this notion of 'freedom' during the war is that for the officer class that produced these memoirs, freedom was associated with the escape *from* the collective living patterns of the prison camps. By contrast, in popular representations of working-class mores during the war, it is that very sense of enforced collectivity which is celebrated as being one of the most important values that emerged as a positive result of the war. Here are two class definitions of 'freedom' that are in complete opposition: in one it is a quality associated with splendid isolation, in another it is associated with the communality of things and the mutual aid of interlocking relationships. The values of such exhortatory films as Humphrey Jennings's *London Can Take It*, emphasizing the collective resistance spirit of working-class London during the Blitz, living together in bomb shelters and all pulling together, is at the opposite end of the pole to the war values exemplified in these accounts of escape and heroic individualism.

Colditz Story is permeated by public-school, officer class values; not surprising in that Colditz was for 'none but officers', particularly those who had already made escape attempts from other camps which Reid himself described as 'prep-schools'. As officers they received fairly moderate treatment and were certainly not expected to work, unlike the majority of prisoners of the Germans incarcerated in labour camps where, as is known, they died or were murdered in their millions once their labour power had been exhausted. In Colditz they ordered a grand piano for their theatre and got it. They frequently refused orders en masse and escaped punishment. These things, though, in no way minimalize the sheer futility and horror of imprisonment without sentence or prospect of release.

Paul Brickhill's *The Great Escape* is a rather more sombre story, for what started out as another escape story from a fairly benevolently run prison camp ends suddenly with the arbitrary execution of the majority of the escapees as a result of the direct orders of Hitler, an act that horrified people in Britain at the time and clearly haunted Brickhill himself. The majority of Brickhill's close colleagues were RAF Officers and public-school educated. The tunnel that was the means of 'the great escape' took nearly a year to dig, and while that was going on some fifty men worked on forging documents, three to five hours a day for the same period. Some eighty prisoners managed to escape and fifty were shot when captured, wherever they were caught.

The RAF officer, shot down over Europe, captured, imprisoned and then escaping, became the archetypal hero of post-war popular literature. To a large extent there was some basis for this in that it was most likely during the first years of the war that it would be airmen who would be captured and imprisoned, since during that period engagements between Britain and Germany took the form of 'the war in the air'. In the second half of the war, however, in North Africa and the Far East, the majority of British casualties and men taken prisoner would have been from the ranks of the Army. Even so, in the Second World War the RAF rapidly became the elite of the three services, and the aviator, or airman, by then had attained an almost mythical status in modern consciousness.

For European writers, but particularly for British writers, the airman was a central figure and symbol in the poetry and prose of the 1920s and 1930s. Yeats's great poem 'An Irish Airman Foresees His Death' was already published in 1919:

> A lonely impulse of delight
> Drove to this tumult in the clouds;
> I balanced all, brought all to mind,
> The years to come seemed waste of breath,
> A waste of breath the years behind
> In balance with this life, this death.

The helmeted figure of the airman also appears in a number of Auden's poems in the 1930s. The lyrical novels of the French aviator and writer Saint-Exupéry were being translated and published during this period too. One of the most disturbing novels published near the beginning of the war was Rex Warner's *The Aerodrome* (1941), which described the takeover of a village by an authoritarian air force based nearby, dedicated to fascistic concepts of efficiency, order and moral discipline. And the poetry that captured most people's imaginations during the war was John Pudney's aircrew poetry, notably 'For Johnny' from his collection *Dispersal Point and Other Air Poems* (1942).

Yet though it is understandable that great heroism was attached to the fighter pilots who were defending the cities against enemy bombing, it seems strange in retrospect that such heroism was attributed to the crews of high-altitude bombers, as against the women and men, for example, who either directly risked their lives in the maintenance of defence and civilian services, as foot soldiers and tank crews in the Western Desert, and as sailors on the North Atlantic convoys. Such men and women were performing equally brave tasks but without being involved in the moral ambiguity of what at times was the necessarily indiscriminate bombing of civilian targets.

After the war an RAF Escaping Society was actually formed, made up of those airmen who had been captured and who had managed to escape back to England. Paul Brickhill's *Escape or Die*, (1954) is a collection of stories about members of that society, published to help raise funds for their post-war work in aiding the families of Europeans who had belonged to resistance networks which had helped escapees get back to England.

Clearly, one of the appeals of the escape books lay in the minutiae of disguise, counterfeit and subterfuge which the escapers employed to get them out of the prison camps and back to their own country. Part of the fascination of prison literature is concerned with how people manage patiently and with great ingenuity to turn tiny resources into major systems of routine survival. The childish fascination with disguise, magical deception and illusionism, is fully addressed in the details of these books. And the ingenuity was astonishing. Eric Williams's companion in *The Wooden Horse* was able to counterfeit work-permits in a couple of hours, reproducing by hand German gothic type, dyeing papers and cardboards with colours rinsed from curtain material, all achieved in a hotel room the night before they had to be used. In Colditz a Polish prisoner constructed a typewriter out of wood, which could be dis-assembled in seconds, and this was used to type out forged documents for would-be escapers. Paul Brickhill has a whole chapter on the work of 'The Forgers' in *The Great Escape*, describing how prisoners worked in production units able to turn out imitation German uniforms, replica guns, workmen's clothes of different nationalities, compasses, headed note-paper and other accessories for the escapers. They also built a duplicator that used the gelatine extracted from invalid jellies and an ink made out of the lead from pencils. And the tunnels they dug were extraordinary achievements of resourcefulness and deception. The interest of all this detail, the iconography of deception and disguise, is, of course, not simply due to a nostalgia for wartime conditions and necessity, because its appeal is also to that sense which every reader has that people can change their identity, change their name, disappear and start a different life somewhere else. Illusionism and masquerade are traditional features of popular theatre and literary forms. The 'escape literature' of the Second World War appealed to that already existing aspect of popular sensibility. Quite a few civilians actually used the social disruption of war to migrate and start new lives.

Heroism in War

By far the largest group of books about the war were those detailing extraordinary fighting missions, or the activities of secret agents where additional resources of courage or daring were required. As such they, too, took on the forms and narrative styles of the popular genres of adventure stories or tales of dangerous exploration. The largest number of them dealt with the accounts of fighter pilots or leaders of audacious bombing expeditions, including Paul Brickhill's *Reach for the Sky* and *The Dam Busters*, Guy Gibson's *Enemy Coast Ahead*, Richard Hillary's *The Last Enemy* and Richard Pape's *Boldness Be My Friend*. These books, together with the RAF prison-escape literature, more than any other war books, provided two of the most important images of the Britain that had gone to war in 1939, and hence the Britain that had to be preserved after the war was over. The first was the evocation of a rural England of country houses, village pubs, public schools, Oxbridge and expensive sports cars. The second was the representation of Britain at war as a second Elizabethan era.

The portrait of England that Eric Williams conjured up was 'the sunshine on the Cambridge countryside and the whiteness of the clouds above'. Of 'driving the Aston Martin fast down the Great North Road in the early morning with the open road long and straight and empty in front of you...' His escaping companion recalls 'Oxford and a houseboat on the Thames...His brother home from Sandhurst; and drinking pints. Janet poling a punt under the green shade of the willows, the water dropping from the pole in a cascade of diamonds and himself lying in a punt and watching her.' H.E. Bates in his introduction to *Escape or Die* described the world the pilots left behind them as one of 'cool beers and English lawns', or breathing the 'calm summer air of an English village'. Guy Gibson evokes a 'peaceful England on a cool spring evening; the flowers are blooming, the hum of serenity is in the air.' Leslie Bell's Lt. Col. Elder Ellis, a senior officer responsible for supplying resistance organizations with weapons, is portrayed at home at the end of the war: 'But if he looks across from his garden he can see silhouetted against the skyline, Windsor Castle itself. It stands there untouched by enemy hands; solid, durable, strangely symbolic of what we have and are....'

To quote these images is in no way to denigrate the courage and achievements of these pilots and their crews; this was the England they had been brought up in and wished to preserve. But it was certainly not everybody's England, or Britain, and hardly any other images of what England or Britain more realistically was appeared in any of the books in paperback that comprised the popular literature of the war. None of the writers registered that there were many versions of Britain, of which their's was only one, and there were simply no accounts by servicemen and women in the ranks of the other Britain. The Britain of mass unemployment, large urban slums, rickets, TB, Relieving Officers, tied cottages, game-keepers and the various other manifestations of a deeply divided class society, simply didn't exist.

It was the short-story writer and novelist, H.E.Bates, who in his introduction to the escape stories collected in *Escape or Die* wrote:

> It has been said, and I think with a great deal of truth, that the RAF were the new Elizabethans, fighting and adventuring in the air, as the great navigators had fought and adventured in the seas.[6]

Bates's most popular novel, *Fair Stood the Wind for France* (1944), was an account of a British bomber crew forced down over France. The title comes from the Elizabethan poem by Michael Drayton 'The Battle of Agincourt'. The same year, of course, saw the showing of Laurence Olivier's *Henry V*, which was consciously made to revive memories of earlier English battles in France and was unapologetically part of the cultural war effort. The film score was by William Walton. *Henry V* has at its centre the Battle of Agincourt and contains that most famous peroration on the British at war, 'Once more unto the breach, dear friends...' But Shakespeare was invoked on many other occasions in this period, not least by the titles that writers chose for their war testimonies. Airey Neave's account of his escape from Colditz was called *They Have Their Exits* (*As You Like It*, Act II, vii, line 141); Richard Pape's story of capture, imprisonment and torture became *Boldness Be My Friend*, (*Cymbeline* Act I, vi, line 18); W. Stanley Moss called his account of the abduction of a key German general from his headquarters in Crete in 1944 *Ill Met By Moonlight* (*Midsummer Night's Dream* Act II, i, line 60).

It is always interesting to observe how a nation in a crisis looks back to an earlier period of history as an exemplar and evocation, a period that matches the political and cultural values which the politicians wish to invoke again. Significantly, much of the literature of the First World War simply wished to reinstate that long Edwardian era which had just been disrupted by the war; there was no long reach back into the past on that occasion, rather a wish simply for the old order to be re-established. The England (not Britain) evoked by the mythology of Agincourt and the rural arcadia of *A Midsummer Night's Dream* was one of robust yeomanry, rustic sensuality and courtly love, as well as the occasional dangerous assignation under the cover of night. In complete contrast, the Conservative government under Margaret Thatcher would rather invoke the self-denying, mercantile values of Victorian economic rapaciousness, coupled with minor works of philanthropy, as a model of the Britain that we should emulate. (Though during the Falklands crisis the press went back rather further in history to find the appropriate imagery for the Navy Task Force that sailed to the Falklands by headlining after the first seamen casualties, Hearts of Oak! This was from the famous sea song of that name that appeared in a pantomime, *Harlequin's Invasion*, first perfomed in 1759 after a year of successful naval victories in the colonies.)

This desire to return to some golden past is, of course, part of the great attraction of conservatism, in that it appears to offer the promise of certainties that have already been tested and proved, as against the rather more painful option of trying to build something new and hitherto untested. What can radicalism offer compared with the imagery of the long Edwardian summers, streets swept clean by deferential working men, well-ordered classrooms, everybody in their place and Britain once again a world power? What was at one time one of the great strengths of the socialist cause—that it had a vision of a new society, an appeal to a new golden age—has foundered in the complexities and realities of industrial and post-industrial society. For actually the vision of the socialist revival of the 1870s onwards, exemplified in Robert Blatchford's bestselling *Merrie England* and in Walter Crane's garlanded figures bringing the harvest home, or dancing round the May-Pole, was itself an appeal to return to a lost commonwealth, an agricultural past that had disappeared. Without a well-worked-out vision of things as they could be, it is not surprising that people will want to revert to things as they were. Because, of course, the present is always unbearable to everybody. Labourism has never come to terms with this crucial problem.

Stories of the Resistance

In his study of European resistance movements during the Second World War M.R.D. Foot writes, 'Resisters tend to be out of step with their time—usually in advance of it...'[7] And it was true that in the resistance movement, many conventional social relations had to be subverted or circumvented. Thus women played a key role and in the literature we are dealing with this is the one category where two of the most popular books dealt with the heroic exploits of women: Jerrard Tickell's *Odette: Story of a British Agent* and Anne-Marie Walters's *Moondrop to Gascony*. But other social relations were subverted too. Those whose work conventionally commanded a low social status—railway workers, shop workers, typists, clerks, garage mechanics—were found to be working in jobs that were strategic and essential to the continuance of everyday life. Because they were, to some extent, socially invisible, this meant they were less likely to be suspected of playing important roles in resistance movements, which many of them did.

Then, too, it is significant that in resistance stories it was impossible not to mention the role of Communist and socialist militants as important activists in these struggles, and this was probably the first time that such militants appeared in a favourable light in popular literature. One also learned through these accounts and testimonies which classes and sections of the society embraced collaboration and which didn't. The literature of resistance was unavoidably political and, quite rarely in popular literature, had to align the forces of good (patriotism, honour, courage) with people such as Communist workers, trade unionists, lower-class workers, itinerant or marginal people such as sailors, prostitutes and criminals, as well as bourgeois nationalists and social-democratic politicians. It was for precisely such reasons of social dislocation that conventional strategists of war such as Sir Basil Liddell Hart have worried about the political implications of recognizing the importance of civilian resistance because the 'social dangers inherent in it, for the future of a settled society.'[8] One of the Dutch resistance slogans encompassed this oppositional ethic: 'Only dead fishes float down the stream, live ones swim against it.'[9]

Oluf Reed Olsen's *Two Eggs On My Plate* (1952) though telling an extraordinary story of hardship, danger and bravery, is one of those resistance because of the 'social dangers inherent in it, for the future of a settled society.'[8] One of the Dutch resistance slogans encompassed this oppositional ethic: 'Only dead fishes float down the stream, live ones swim against it.'[9]

harrowing boat journey of fourteen days. He returned one and a half years later covertly and played a key role in the Norwegian resistance until the end of the war in 1945. The reader is given no understanding of the nature of the social system that occupied and subjected Norway to totalitarian rule: the Germans are simply...the Germans.

This is true also of such books as MacGregor Urquhart's *Partisan*, the story of an escaped British POW who joined the Italian resistance and the cover blurb of which summarizes completely the narrative ideology of that account: 'This is a nerve-tearing tale of hard combat in Tunisia and imprisonment in Italy, followed by a wildly exciting life on the run in company with the Italian partisans. It is crammed with hard dramatic action and spine-chilling crises so cannot fail to enthrall even the most shock-hardened reader.' Similarly, a book such as Gunby Hadath's *Men of the Maquis* (1947) is told as a series of audacious adventure stories in which the enemy appear to be just other individuals, 'les Boches' rather than fascists. The word 'fascism' simply *never appears* in any of the many books that make up that extensive literature of the war which appeared in paperback. Whether this was because keen editors were apt to pencil out any passages of attempted political analysis by the narrators—in case it bogged down the fast flow of the narative—or because the writers had self-censored themselves in advance in deference to narrow notions about the ingredients of successful stories we do not know.

Anne-Marie Walters's *Moondrop to Gascony* is rather different in that her story of her work as a British secret agent in France is as much a reflection on her own sense of what her life was being lived for as it is an account of clandestine espionage activities. Her account contains a number of perorations on her own mental states, her sense of having no other choices in a war in which fascism for a long time appeared to be able to win and her fears of death, and these qualities make it all the more moving. Although Anne-Marie Walters's account was that of a British subject, she was of English-French parentage. Hardly any French and Italian accounts of resistance were translated and published widely in Britain. What were translated after the war were those fictional accounts such as Jean-Paul Sartre's trilogy *The Roads to Freedom*, Simone de Beauvoir's *The Blood of Others* and Camus's allegory *The Plague*. These developed the experience of the resistance into the post-war political and cultural aesthetic of 'existentialism', which there is no doubt was quite deeply influential as a cultural mood in many European countries and extended far beyond that of being a mere coterie fashion. Certainly Sartre, de Beauvoir and Camus were very widely read in Britain, much more so than the majority of British novelists writing at the time, and this was largely because no British writers (with a couple of exceptions to be discussed later) developed any political/literary aesthetic out of the experience of that major historical nightmare, the fascist occupation of central Europe.

The Literature of the Holocaust

'After Auschwitz,' Theodor Adorno wrote, 'there can be no more poetry.'

Yet there had to be writing, otherwise only a few people would ever know exactly what happened in the concentration camps in Europe and the prisoner-of-war camps run by the Japanese in Malaya and Burma. Of all the genres of war literature it is the literature of the camps which continues to exercise a compulsive fascination and morbidity. Such books as *Scourge of the Swastika*, *The Naked Island* and more poignantly, *The Diary of Anne Frank*, continue to be reprinted, as I personally feel they should be, even though it has always been apparent that on many occasions such books have been read—and even promoted through the imagery of the book-covers—as part of the pornography of sadism.

One of the first accounts published in Britain by a survivor of the Buchenwald camp was *The Dungeon Democracy* (1945) by Christopher Burney. It remains a mystery why this was never published in paperback and promoted in the 1950s as so many others were, since it is a very rare account by a British soldier of the experience of one of the concentration camps. But Burney himself predicted a later flood of books after his own, full of 'words of self-righteousness', whereas Burney's account is not so much anti-German or anti-Nazi, as rather completely pessimistic about humanity per se. For the book has a theme—which is that the prisoners at Buchenwald could have organized themselves into a united body of resistance, but they failed to do so. In Burney's account the prisoners stuck together in groups on the basis of nationality and simply fended for themselves. This question of why there was so little resistance in the camps was in fact raised later on and became quite contentious (and also a little anti-Semitic once again), for it revived that commonplace political tactic of blaming the victims for being victims. Burney's account actually doesn't do this; for him the terrifying thing about Buchenwald was that it revealed how superficial notions of individual morality actually were, and how rapidly people would accede to the exigencies of other environments.

Strangely, a later book by Burney, *Solitary Confinement* (1952), an account of his capture in France as a British agent and his year in solitary confinement before being sent to Buchenwald, did get published in paperback and went through a number of editions. This was much more in the tradition of the genre of prison literature, being mostly a series of reflections on loneliness, isolation and human self-sufficiency. Russell Braddon's, *The Naked Island*, first published in 1952 and still in print is the best-known account of life as a Japanese prisoner-of-war. While the Japanese did not have a programme of mass murder of prisoners as did the Nazi regime, many thousands of prisoners died as a result of exhaustion through forced labour and the lack of any kind of care through adequate diet or living conditions. Braddon does raise one of the few questions in these books that refers to class inequalities back in Britain, which otherwise appears as the embodiment of everything that is best and perfect in a nation. He reports that the British prisoners died much more easily of dysentry than the fitter, healthier Australians who had enjoyed a much better standard of living as civilians before the war. The health of many of the British soldiers was in fact poor when they had joined up as a result of class poverty in the Britain of the 1930s. But Braddon's account is fuelled by a terrible racism which, though understandable at the time when it was first written, remains uncorrected or unmodified in subsequent editions—the war 'of Asia against the white man' will go on forever and is in Braddon's terms endemic. One can only assume that he had not then read any accounts of the Nazi atrocities performed in the name of an ideology which was that of 'the white man' carried to its genetic extremes.

The most comprehensive account of the horrors of German fascism was *The Scourge of the Swastika: A Short History of Nazi War Crimes* by Lord Russell of Liverpool, first published in 1954 and more or less reprinted and reissued every year since then. It is described by its author in the preface as being 'intended to provide the ordinary reader with a truthful and accurate account of many of these German war crimes. It has been compiled from the evidence given and the documents produced at various war-crime trials, and from statements made by eye-witnesses of war crimes to competent war-crime investigation commissions in the countries where they were committed.' I had always been prejudiced against this book, mostly because I believed it was read as a kind of pornography, and I suspected the intentions of the writer and its publishers. In fact, re-reading it today, I believe it is a sober and genuinely horrified account, nightmarish in its details, whose publication has been consistently justified.

More worrying was the treatment of women's accounts of the camps, such as Micheline Maurel's *Ravensbruck* (1958) and *House of Dolls* (1956) by Ka-Tzetnik 135633, which were published in ways that framed them as part of the pornography of sadism. Micheline Maurel's book, sincerely and despairingly written, has on its cover a full-breasted woman in a skimpy dress with pouting red lips pressed against a barbed wire fence. The *House of Dolls* emphasizes that it is a story of enforced prostitution and on the front cover has the words, 'It shows the depths of bestiality to which Germans sank under Hitler...' In both cases the publishing format itself contributes to the ambiguity of motive with which such books could be read.

Yet the book that remains the most poignant and searing of all has also been the most popular—*The Diary of Anne Frank*, first published in Britain in 1953 and in its 45th printing in 1981, suggesting that once again people find it difficult to encompass tragedy and barbarism on a huge scale and have to find its meaning through the plight of an individual, and through that most personal of forms, the diary. And, paradoxically, there is something about a diary entry with its absolute specificity of date and place, that recreates the writer again at the moment of reading more than any other form, whereas more general attempts to create 'timelessness' in writing, date so much more rapidly. On a number of occasions when I have read this diary, in private, or with a class of school-students, as I begin at the first entry it is as if the war were beginning again, and as I read on I just hope that with this reading Anne Frank remains undiscovered in her secret room and survives; such is the power of the diary form.

Thus all these various kinds of war literature developed into specific genres for that period and after that slowly fed back into other mainstream genres of popular literature: prison literature, male heroism, resistance and politics, and the new one of Nazi revivalism. Two of these genres have dominated male popular literature ever since the work of such writers as Alistair MacLean, whose first novel, HMS *Ulysses*, was set on a ship escorting a Russian convoy through the North Sea and around the Artic during one winter of the war. Since then all MacLean's novels, almost all set in exclusively male settings—a nuclear submarine, an oil rig, a commando squad—have been popular bestsellers, seventeen of them selling over one million copies each, and have made him, according to John Sutherland[10], the bestselling English novelist ever'.

More disturbing have been the consistently popular novels of writers such as H. H. Kirst, Sven Hassell, and Leon Kessler, all of whom produce violent war books based on the exploits of German commando units with such titles as *Cauldron of Blood, Slaughter Ground, Otto's Blitzkrieg*, that suggest a good wallow in the mire. Slightly more sophisticated, but still banking on a morbid fascination with the excesses of Hitler's Third Reich, have been novels fantasizing secret plots to short-circuit the war such as Jack Higgins's *The Eagle Has Landed*, built around the idea of an audacious German plot to kidnap Winston Churchill, and a number of others detailed in Sutherland's two chapters on war fiction in *Bestsellers*.

Three Dissenting Writers

Yet now it is important to look at a handful of books about the war that were not promoted in these popular ways, even though they contributed some of the most powerful writing to have emerged from that experience. Alexander Baron's *From the City, From the Plough* (1948) has already been mentioned. Many reviewers at the time considered it possibly the best novel about the war written by a British writer. *The Daily Worker* described it as 'the finest book to appear in Britain concerning the Second World War'. V.S.Pritchett, doyen of novel reviewers, thought it 'the only war book that has conveyed any sense of reality to me'. Baron, East London born, Jewish, Labour League of Youth organizer and, in 1946, demobbed soldier, wrote this very fine novel at nights. 'It was partly something I had to get off my chest and partly because after the war the first few novels to get published were all by officers, or by the kind of intellectuals to whom the army was an agony...'

From the City, From the Plough is set in an army camp on the South Downs as one battalion waits for the invasion of Normandy to begin, when they will be landed in France to start the final offensive against the Germans. All of Baron's characters are working-class men, fully developed figures mostly, and he allows them to talk about their civilian lives and the conditions of life and work they have come from before the army. Here is a portrait of a Britain that simply isn't there in most of the other books: the struggle for survival in the major cities against slum housing, casual labour, poor health and little hope for the future. There are also those who have come from the rural areas where, as labourers, they and their parents before them have been worked to exhaustion on the land in order to earn the means of survival only. In Baron's male community there are no heroics, for a change, no great masculine virtues, but rather a group of men thrown together, learning to live with each other, many of them frightened, many of them making the best out of a situation which they no longer control. They comfort each other, sort out squabbles, try to learn to live communally—and wait. The battle scenes that follow the final landing are horrendous, more shocking than any others I have read, and only a handful survive. The values that emanate from Baron's book are not those of some mythologized 'England' or specious nationalism, but of a class that puts the welfare of others, mutual support and solidarity, above the values of individualism and self-interest. Whereas the heroes of so much popular war literature are always shown to be fighting in order to preserve the past, the men in *From the City, From the Plough* are shown to be fighting for a different future.

After *From the City, From the Plough* Baron wrote three more books about the war: *There's No Home* (1950) deals with a brief interlude between the fighting for a group of British soldiers in Sicily; *With Hope, Farewell* (1952) is the story of a young Jewish pilot who is badly injured in a crash and who cannot settle down to civilian life after the war; and a very fine collection of short stories, *The Human Kind* (1953), is built around small incidents in people's lives just before, during and just after the war. A lot of detail in these stories is concerned with the traumas of fighting and the social dislocation caused by the war, and the problem, particularly for men, of re-building a 'post-war self'. In these stories, for a change, there is no false sentimentality or Little Englandism. In one very powerful story, 'Scum of the Earth', a drunken squaddie pours out a monologue of hate against all foreigners, the 'Wogs' and the 'Wops', to whom 'It's no use talking, it's only your fist they understand.' He goes on to recount in great detail his rape and humiliation of the young Italian girl he found rifling the dustbins of the camp for food, and continues by inveighing against *her* degradation and sexual promiscuity. Jingoism, ignorance and sadism are all combined in a horrible portrait of British arrogance and self-righteousness. But there are also very moving stories of human decency and self-effacing generosity, particularly in the ranks.

The work of Dan Billany is even less known than that of Baron, yet his two books about the war are possibly the most moving of all. Little is known about Billany other than that he died in an Italian prisoner-of-war camp 'in an attempt to stop the activities of a British informer', probably in 1944. The manuscripts of the two books he wrote, written while he was a prisoner were given to an Italian farmer (presumably by Billany himself) who after the war sent them on to Billany's parents, who in turn sent them to the publishers.

Dan Billany attended an elementary school in Hull which he left in 1928. His first job was as an errand boy. Three years later he attended some classes for unemployed young people and went on to pass sufficient examinations to be able to go to Hull University from 1934 to 1937. He became an English teacher and on the outbreak of war joined 'C'

Company of the 4th Battalion, East Yorkshire Regiment which was posted to North Africa in 1942 and which, on 1 June that year, came under severe attack from Rommel's Eighth Army with many British soldiers being taken prisoner, including Billany. They were taken to Italy where they were put into prison camps. It was in his prison camp that Billany wrote *The Trap* and, with the collaboration of another prisoner, David Dowie, *The Cage*. The order in which they were written remains unknown, but *The Cage* was published first, in 1949, when, as it says on the book cover, 'the fates of the two authors' were still unknown.

In the introduction to *The Cage* Billany and Dowie argued for the importance of writing directly about their situation: 'If we delayed writing till we got back to England we should gain in tranquillity, but in everything else we should lose.' The style of the book is unusual in that it is made up of short episodes, discussions on paper between the two writers, portraits of other prisoners, and, in the final section, the story of an infatuation between two men, a love for each other that is denied by both any form of physical expression. Unlike most other portraits of prison camp life, *The Cage* consciously lacks any individual heroics and is deeply analytical of the disturbing shifts and pressures of prison camp life (including the breakdown of traditional 'masculine' values). It ignores the possibility of escape in preference to reflections on the question of the larger prison beyond the camp walls. The authors even suggest that their prison experience has freed them from some things:

> Soon now we shall go out from here—back into the world. How many of us will be truly freed—none, I suppose. But some must have gained a certain freedom from prison; the prison of walls and wire must have helped them out of the prison of mistrust.

Billany's hand is often recognizable by its political acuity and fondness for striking metaphors and aphorisms that give the singly written novel, *The Trap*, its incredible strength. In one of the entries in *The Cage*, Billany describes the relationship between fascism and the architecture of the local orphanage where they are being kept temporarily, a building erected in the era of Mussolini's state programme:

> Exit the sham-eternal, Fontanello Orphanage, type of Fascism. Hundreds of tons of extraneous masonry piled along the facade, but the whole building shakes when a few people jump on an upstairs floor...it looks like the Parthenon, but it will vanish in the night. And even so it will outlast the

Fascism that built it, and children whose parents have been killed by Fascism will trace their shadowed lives back to this cheap building. Pretension. The attempt to freeze the flow of life, to impose a pattern on events. Reality laughs at such attempts. You can't cage the future, it will have its way. To build a rigid social system which would last forever, what a hope. The only thing that never changes is Change.

However, I believe that *The Trap* is Billany's most important book (he had published two short novels before the war). It is a tragic novel about the break-up of relatively settled, though harsh, patterns of working-class life by the advent of war, and the prospect of permanent cultural fragmentation. The first two-thirds of the novel concern the love affair between the narrator, a young middle-class officer, and a working-class woman, Elizabeth. They marry before he leaves for Africa, and the last third of the novel concerns his experience of the desert war and his capture by the Germans and Italians. The novel ends with the narrator's arrival in an Italian prison camp.

The context of much of the first part of the novel is the family life of Elizabeth, and it is Billany's attempt to portray the material difficulties of working-class life in the 1930s in Britain. The characters are well realized, the story flows, with intervening moments of personal and social tragedy as the war bites into the lives of the families in the town where the narrator is stationed. Yet what gives *The Trap* its lasting status as a highly original and political novel is the reflectiveness and aphoristic quality of the writing. When the narrator interrupts the narrative to address the reader, as Billany does often in *The Trap*, one is reminded very much of a sensibility strangely similar to Walter Benjamin's. Two such aphorisms about history that are found in *The Trap* might well have come from Benjamin:

> But our eyes. They will reveal our blight to the future—Unfilled Hope. Eternal Hope. Unrealized Hope. We only live in Hope: in hope that tomorrow will give us that unknown satisfaction which, yesterday, Hope expected today.... The Present is a room; the Past furnishes it, the Future lights it.

Much of the third chapter of the novel is made up of a lengthy peroration by Billany on the way in which the working class has been portrayed historically in the novel:

> It used to be the fashion to see the working class always from a little distance—if not through bars, at least through an impervious psychological

> screen, so that their actions and emotions were as irrelevant to the gentle
> Writer and the gentle Reader as those of flatfish on the floor of their
> aquarium, on the other side of their thick glass and in their own bottle-
> green element.
>
> As examples of Humble Worth, the working class at one time challenged
> the dog... (As a literary device)

One can understand how such insights set Billany's work very much
against the conventions of popular war literature in which the other ranks
still functioned as a foil to the individual achievements of their officers.

The achievement of *The Trap* is that it manages to combine many
usually separate genres and modes of writing while remaining an in-
tegrated whole. It is certainly a very moving and by no means sentimental
love story; it is also a novel of working-class family life shattered by war;
it is a war novel, too, and a genuinely frightening one; but it is also a
novel about writing a novel, about how to write a novel (under prison
conditions) that is a political polemic and an intervention into questions
of literary aesthetics. And towards the end biting questions about im-
perialist ideologies and their rationalizations are asked (ideologies that un-
consciously informed many other books about the campaign in North
Africa and the Far East). Writing of some Egyptian peasants, the narrator
asks the reader to see that,

> ...those that destroyed them, mocked them. They that wasted them,
> demanded of them a song. To their foul injury they added foul insult—trod
> them into the dung, then called them 'dirty Wogs': starved them till their
> ribs showed white, and so that their children's shins were no thicker than a
> stick of celery—so that they prayed for even a crust—then 'all Wogs are
> beggars': kicked them till they flinched at a shadow—'shifty Wogs': robbed
> them till there was nothing but their breath to steal, then 'every Wog is a
> thief...'[13]

It seems to me to be the finest novel to come out of the war, yet it has
been largely forgotten. It was published by Faber in 1950 and reissued by
the Readers' Union in 1952. It was republished in 1974 by Cedric
Chivers, but has only ever appeared in hard-back and remains a book
known only to a minority. That kind of publishing history is also very
much a part of the way in which the war has been reconstructed in
popular literature since 1945, the way in which really significant books
such as Billany's have been both marginalized and in some ways silenced.

The last of our books to have substantially rejected the mythology of war is Stuart Hood's *Pebbles From My Skull* (1963). This was clearly written as a result of a return visit by Hood to the region of Italy where he had been an escaped prisoner on the run some twenty years earlier. It is both a reconstruction of that period and an inquiry into his own understanding of that experience. For again, here there is no heroic, selfless flight immediately back to England, but instead an interest in the country in which he found himself free and on the run. Hood, in fact, spent from 8 September 1943 until 15 August 1944, nearly one whole year, at large in the hills and valleys of Chianti, sometimes fighting with the partisans, often on his own, 'taking time out of life'. There are many similarities with Billany's experience. Hood found life outside prison form many people, particularly the peasants, actually harder than inside, because existence was totally 'tied to a cycle of labour, and life mean, squalid, hard', where some even looked forward to death and a release. In such accounts there are no abstract notions of 'freedom' as some metaphysical quality that exists over and above the actual material reality of day-to-day life—there is just a variety of circumstances in which people struggle to create various kinds of freedoms.

Among the partisans that Hood fought with were Russian and Yugoslavian Communists, a rare portrait in war literature of an internationalism that transcended specific national interests.

Among the peasants in what became German-occupied Italy, Hood found the women braver than the men, but also found that effective resistance, or guerrilla struggles, were often as cruel in their methods and choices as those of the enemy they fought. And in saying this Hood, in the only reference in the book to the period in which it was written, suggests that readers might bear this in mind when thinking about the 'terrorist' struggles that were then being waged in Cyprus against the British forces. The book concludes with a most moving series of passages about what Hood learned from his 'time out of life', of his understanding of what was still then an unchanging pattern of peasant life, culture and death, and the many examples of human selflessness that strangers showed him.

These three writers then, Baron, Billany and Hood, were able to achieve a literature of the Second World War that went against the grain of most of the conventionally published and promoted popular literature. They are the only writers with whom one can begin to compare the far more angular and tough-minded realism of the best of the American novels about the war, particularly Norman Mailer's *The Naked and the*

Dead, James Jones's *From Here to Eternity* and, more recently, Kurt Vonnegut's *Slaughterhouse 5*. The American writers at least acknowledged that what was being fought towards the end of the Second World War was no longer a war of soldiers and rifles but a technological war of saturation bombing, fire-bombing and the first use of atomic weapons—'total war' as we now understand it.

The majority of popular writing about the war published in Britain never came near an understanding of this. It is significant that the great wave of books appeared some considerable time after the war actually ended, in most cases six or seven years after. This is a little strange. Yet without being conspiratorial, it is not difficult to see that the political climate of the early 1950s was becoming rapidly different from that which had surrounded the end of the war and the General Election of 1945. Then, there had been an air of radical change around, a feeling of going forward to an alternative society. Yet with the return of a Conservative Government in 1951, after a long period of Labour rationing and austerity, the political atmosphere was already in retreat, beginning to look back again. And a war that had been fought in the name of anti-fascism and which had ended with a call for radical change at home, was by then already in the process of being reconstructed as a war to preserve the old order. It was no doubt easier to find a publisher for these books once that mood had changed, and the success of each book—and the great wave of this literature really only gets going after 1951—added further impetus to the publication of more like them. They caught a change of mood, but they also helped to form and historicize it. Popular literature is one of the most important ways of achieving the reconstruction of popular history.

The 'meaning' of the Second World War is very much with us again today. The Conservative Party, and particularly the Prime Minister, Margaret Thatcher, have begun to invoke the Churchillian era and rhetoric as belonging to a war which 'they' won, and have effectively buried the radical movements and currents that eddied through both the civilian and service populations at the time. And the mythology of that war is now being used, ironically, as a means of attacking the contemporary peace movement in Britain. 'What strengthens my conservatism,' the historian Lord Beloff recently wrote, 'is that for me a CND badge and a swastika are essentially interchangeable.' And recently CND demonstrations have been barracked by 'Atlanticist'-funded movements trying to drown out speeches by the playing of patriotic music. The theme from the film *The Dam Busters*, based on Paul Brickhill's reconstruction of that bombing raid, is now the most often heard. It seems that Britain's part in the Second World War will have to be fought all over again—on paper, that is—if its radical meanings are to be recaptured for the present.

Writing

4
Expressionism and Working-Class Fiction

In his essay, 'The Storyteller', Walter Benjamin distinguishes between two generic traditions of story-telling, symbolized by two contrasting occupations: the peasant and the voyager. 'If one wants to picture these two groups through their archaic representatives', he wrote, 'one is embodied in the resident tiller of the soil, and the other in the trading seaman.'[1] One told the stories of the village, its people and its history, while the other brought stories from lands where people lived different lives according to different customs. Both traditions complemented each other. Benjamin's distinction remains valuable in contemporary arguments about finding cultural forms and processes which enable the balancing of the local and particular with the national and international. This is one of the most pressing contemporary political and cultural problems and currently finds its most developed expression in the controversies surrounding the achievements—and also the limitations—of the recent and widespread growth of local people's history projects.[2] This distinction is also useful to employ when looking back at one of the most energetic periods of working-class writing, the 1930s, because by doing so it becomes clear that most recent attention to the writing of that decade has been focused on just one of the traditions—the local—at the expense of understanding attempts to create a different aesthetic of working-class experience based not on place and continuity but on dislocation and transience.

For when we think of the working-class writers of the 1930s who made a permanent and popular impact, we think of the writers who took as their political and aesthetic ambition the project of describing the life of the communities they lived in, usually employing a literary technique most easily summarized as 'documentary realism'. The writers and books of that period whose names and titles are still recalled today would include for example, Walter Brierley with *Means Test Man*, B. L. Coombes with *These Poor Hands*, Willy Goldman with *East End My Cradle*, Walter Greenwood with *Love on the Dole*, Lewis Jones with *Cwmardy* and *We Live*, and John Sommerfield with *May Day*. (Lewis Grassic Gibbon's *A Scot's Quair* is, I personally feel, a quite singular and separate achievement in that decade.) All of these books were essentially literary documents rooted in the continuity of class and *place*. Not surprisingly they emanated from communities with strong local identities often occasioned by the predominance of a single local industry. Brierley was a Derbyshire miner; Coombes and Jones both worked in South Wales pits (though Coombes had experienced one dislocation of place in the move from Herefordshire to South Wales as a teenager in search of work); Greenwood wrote from the experience of life in industrial Salford; Goldman of life in the Jewish East End; and Sommerfield about the tightly-knit working-class districts of riverside London.

In such books the communities in which they are set are whole worlds in themselves and little reference is made to events, places and peoples beyond them. Continuity of employment, even in the same pit or factory as the father, is one kind of ambition either realized or thwarted by the recession and large-scale unemployment. Continuity also of family life along the old patterns is also often represented as an ideal, sometimes achieved but often disrupted as liaisons go amiss and become the major sources of drama in the novels. The desire to affirm the significance of the everyday life in the pit villages and industrial towns of what was still 'Unknown England' was encouraged by the developing oppositional aesthetics of that period. The poetry of Auden, Spender, C.Day-Lewis and MacNeice explored the imagery of the derelict industrial North. Literary and journalistic figures like Middleton-Murray, John Lehmann and George Orwell were always keen to commission documentary reporting by workers of their conditions; and, of course, Mass Observation developed the particularity of place and time to the extent that the degree of detail became self-parodying. (In his report on 'The Pub and The People', one Mass Observer spent an evening in a Bolton pub counting how many times the spittoon was used each hour by different customers smoking different cigarettes and drinking different drinks!) Family life, then, was portrayed as the natural cell of the working-class community, and the permanent continuity of place and employment were the buttresses needed to ensure that family life continued as it should.

A Different 'Proletarian' Fiction

But such experience of class were by no means universal. For the many people brought up in single industry communities, with strong local traditions, there were as many for whom class was experienced as the dislocation of the generations, the rootlessness of city life, a succession of casual jobs and the constant search for employment—often involving moving from town to town. There was also often extreme psychological isolation. Such people, or at least the men among them, might have found some of their feeling and experiences represented in the work of three Liverpool-Irish writers of the 1920s and 1930s—George Garrett, James Hanley and Jim Phelan—who, with the exception of Hanley, have been largely forgotten. Yet for a time they were clearly developing a quite different tradition of working-class or 'proletarian' literature, not unconnected with the fact that they were all completely displaced from settled working-class communities. Like Benjamin's other archaic representative of a different story-telling tradition, Garret, Hanley and Phelan were all seamen.

Phelan and Garrett certainly knew each other and met from time to time between voyages to have a drink and talk about books and writing. In his autobiography, *The Name's Phelan*, Jim Phelan recalled such meetings: 'One of the most enlivening experiences of those days was that I met Joe Jarrett (George Garrett) twice, in the intervals of his sea-going. He too had become a big, broad-shouldered fellow, was very certain of himself, and we behaved like two schoolboys when we met. To my surprise, he thought and spoke of himself as a writer, although nine-tenths of his time was spent in the stoke-holds. Some of his stories were published, and one or two long poems—we drank the money down Bootle dock road.'[3] Hanley knew of them but never met them, but they could hardly have been unaware of his writings since his first novels published in the first half of the 1930s were all set among Liverpool-Irish dockside families or featured the same kind of men at sea. They were also all at different times contributing stories and articles to magazines like *The Adelphi*, *New Writing* and *Left Review*, and so would have been aware of each other's work.

Now while the links between these three men were so tenuous that one cannot properly regard them as having formed a conscious 'school' of proletarian writing, neither should one try to understand their work only as the separate achievements of three different writers who happened to be at work in the same city during the same period. There are many similarities of theme, technical experimentation and acknowledgements of literary influences that make it possible to read their work together with greater insight than if read separately. Apart from the fact that all three had worked as seamen, they all shared a very deep interest in the expressionist drama of Ibsen, Strindberg and O'Neill which led them to explore non-realist forms of fictionalizing working-class life (which Hanley has continued to do up until the present day, sadly without the recognition his work deserves).

1. James Hanley

James Hanley was the first of these writers to be published. His first novel, *Drift*, came out in 1930. He was born in 1901 in a Merseyside Catholic family and went to sea at the age of fourteen. He remained at sea for nine years, an avid reader by his own account all the while, and when he returned to life on shore permanently he settled with the idea of becoming a writer. *Drift* explored many of the themes to which he—and Garrett and Phelan—returned to time and time again. The novel tells the story of a young boy, Joe, who refuses to follow his father into work as a seaman on leaving school, and is shown to be less than enthusiastic about any kind of work at all. Already this represents a break from the pervasive notions of continuity of experience which characterize the major tendency of working-class novels in the 1930s. Joe is determined to find a different way of life to that of his parents, relations and neighbours, whom he regards as permanently trapped in a fixed cycle of exploited labour as well as emotionally under-developed as a result of living under a terrible religious tyranny. Joe experiences Liverpool not as a free and easy seaport town where material poverty was compensated for by communal solidarity, but as an expressionistic nightmare: 'And always ascending towards the heavens the clouds of smoke and grease and steam. The city was heaving up its guts. There it lay like some huge beast. Meanwhile Joe was tramping along in the direction of the river. The pavements were aflood with life. And the cold tang of dawn—one saw it in the pinched blue faces. On they swept. Swarming miraculous life. The human ambulance, a mighty phalanx sweeping down, down, down.'

joe is viewed with deep mistrust by the rest of his family for both spurning loyalty to the Catholic Church and for reading the 'disgusting and atheistical' works of Zola and Joyce. Worse still he is carrying on an affair with a young prostitute. Sexuality, particularly adolescent sexuality, looms ominously in many of Hanley's novels. Sexuality is 'an abyss of desire' which is likely to consume and devour. It stands in opposition to the declared values of proper family life and therefore can only be found away from the community in the twilight world of those who have rejected (or have been rejected by) the puritan certainties of those working-class communities where religion is a much more powerful ingredient of consciousness than are the material exigencies of class. Towards the end of the novel Joe is waiting in Lime Street hoping to catch sight of Jane, the prostitute he is infatuated with, and through his eyes the reader observes the relentless parade of misery and ugliness which is likely to finally overpower him: the bulls being driven down to the abattoir, the prostitutes with their intoxicated, blowzy charms, the drunks and vagrants, the ragged and hungry children, the hellfire soap box orators. Neither land nor sea offer anything of value or possibility to Joe as he thinks about his future life. Society is a deranged nightmare.

Socialist politics enter the novel only briefly, represented by the least convincing of any of the characters in *Drift*. The socialists are portrayed as middle and upper-class aesthetes who lounge about in each other's flats listening to Beethoven and talking about Tolstoy and modern sculpture. Such a portrait was clearly a deliberate misrepresentation by Hanley, for there certainly was a strong working-class socialist tradition in Liverpool in the 1920s and 1930s; Hanley obviously wanted to emphasize Joe's helpless position for which the expressionistic style was the most suitable. And expressionism is a way of portraying the process of crisis, not a way of formulating possible solutions. Joyce's Stephen Daedalus is very much a prototype for Hanley's Joe, but Hanley was remarkably successful in creating a convincing Liverpool dockland milieu for his character, and the twin daemonologies of religion and sexuality are portrayed with great power and authenticity. It must have been a shocking and disturbing book to have published in 1930. And for a first novel a forceful achievement.

Boy and *The Furys*

Even more shocking, however, was Hanley's next novel, *Boy*, published in 1931, which remains the work by which Hanley is best known. It went through three very rapid reprints and was then banned for obscenity in

1932, since when it has never been re-published. It is dedicated to Nancy Cunard, the shipping heiress who became very involved in the world of avant-garde art in the 1920s and, later, left-wing cultural politics in the 1930s. It was Nancy Cunard who organized the famous edition of *Left Review* in 1937 which was called 'Authors Take Sides' and published the results of a widely distributed questionnaire on well-known writers' attitudes to the Spanish Civil War. The dedication also suggests something of the way in which relatively unknown working-class writers were able to get published in that period. It happened mostly by political patronage from left-wing people active in metropolitan literary life. Hanley was certainly encouraged and supported by Cunard and John Lehmann; Garrett by Middleton-Murray, Lehmann and Orwell; Phelan by H.G. Wells.

Boy is a truly disturbing novel. It opens in the classroom of a slum school where a young boy is about to tell the headmaster that his parents have decided that he must leave school to go to work. The boy himself would like to stay on (like the main character in *Drift* he is positively terrified of having to join the treadmill of slum life and toil on which his parents have wasted their lives), but he is completely at the mercy of his tyrannical parents. The headmaster sees education as offering no hope to the working class confronted by the demands of the economic system, 'this huge machine that daily ground people's hopes beneath its wheels'. Any resistance at home to his father's decision to get him a job at the docks is met by being beaten into senselessness while his mother looks on indifferently, her mind on the additional income which the boy's wages will bring into the house. Working-class male self-assertion and violence are portrayed by Hanley with great disgust and bitterness.

The novel, very simply written, gains a powerful allegorical weight by being quite unspecific about its geographical location. It is simply set in a 'dockside community' of unmediated bleakness and despair. The young boy is placed in work by his father, and his first day's work inside the docks is spent baling out the bilges of a ship, standing up to his armpits in fouled water passing up buckets to another young boy at the top of the ladder. Later in the day he is put to work scaling out the inside of the ship's boilers with another team of boys, chipping away in darkness and oppressive heat at the coke deposits left on the boiler walls. As it is his first day the other boys decide he will have to be 'initiated', a process of being tied up, covered in paint and locked in one of the boilers. Overhearing these plans he runs away and decides on the spot to stow away on another ship about to leave that night. All the other young boys are shown by Hanley to have been rapidly brutalized by the conditions of work and trapped in a very callous and aggresive working-class masculinity.

So the boy hides in the coke–hold of the ship where he quickly becomes very ill and feverish through lack of food, general ill-health and sheer moral terror. He is discovered by one of the seamen who takes him to his cabin, puts the boy to bed and then rapes him. This scene is made all the more powerful by the fact that in the original edition about every third word for the duration of this scene is represented by a series of asterisks. In the morning the captain is notified of the boy's presence and it is agreed that he be allowed to work his passage until the ship returns to England. As the voyage progresses he is bullied and sexually assaulted by a number of members of the crew and his mind becomes increasingly suffused with an enormous horror of life. They arrive at a port in the Middle East for a short stay and the boy is taken by an older sailor to a brothel where the boy becomes infatuated with the young prostitute he is offered. In these novels only prostitutes represent female sexuality. The terrors of adolescent sexuality are again portrayed with power: the rigidities of a particular kind of religious character formation make sexuality, or 'lust' as it is described, a very self-destructive process. The boy contracts syphilis and falls into a violent fever back on board and his mind becomes completely deranged. The captain in a moment of pity goes to him one evening, lays his greatcoat over the boy's face and smothers him to death. The whole action of the novel, from schoolroom to death-bed, takes place within perhaps ten days; and the pace of the novel accelerates as it goes along so that the shock of the boy's death at the end is very powerful indeed. Such a novel could have been written only by a person who knew life on board ships in all its squalid tyranny and oppressiveness, and by someone who was, as Hanley described himself, 'drenched in Strindberg, Synge and Ibsen.' One might be more direct and say that *Boy*, has many structural and thematic similarities to Ibsen's *Ghosts*.

In 1935 Hanley published *The Furys*, a very long and panoramic novel of working-class family life in Liverpool centred around the Fury family, hence the title. Once again this family, or 'workers' dynasty' as Soviet critics have come to call this kind of novel, is centred around the whims and wishes of the father, Denny Fury. Denny has been a sailor for most of his life, but has been encouraged to stay at home and oversee the family as they grow into adulthood. Denny feels trapped on land, and, like many other characters in the novels and stories of Hanley, Garrett and Phelan,

dreams of taking a ship as a way of escaping the responsibilities and oppressive relationship of everyday social life. Here these writers are looking
at certain possibilities of escape from the exigencies of class oppression
which the working-class writers of locality and place did not recognize. In
Boy the young main character had sought escape unsuccessfully in his
case—by taking a boat. In *The Furys* Denny is shown early in the novel
'floating about the city like a cork upon water, waiting and hoping for
some release. Only a ship could deliver him.'

Once again the novel focuses on the young son—Peter—who has
returned home after a period of some years in Ireland training for the
priesthood. He has failed to take Orders, to the enormous disappointment
of his mother, who had great hopes of her favourite son becoming a
priest, a powerful sentiment in many working-class Catholic families.
Peter returns to Liverpool dissatisfied with his life and determined not to
get trapped in the way of life of his parents and other brothers and sisters.
Peter is the uncommitted observer in the novel, wandering through the
bleak and loveless city and through other people's lives as the young
Stephen D. wanders through Joyce's *Ulysses*. He witnesses the large
demonstrations of the Liverpool unemployed and their brutal suppression by the the police (described at length by George Garrett in *Liverpool
1921-1922* and later by Jim Phelan in *Ten-A-Penny-People*). He is also
picked up by the Mephistophelean Professor Titmouse, an ominous and
homosexual figure of terrifying visions. He inveigles himself into becoming the lover of his sister-in-law, an attractive woman estranged from her
husband Desmond, an active socialist and railway worker, always out at
meetings or at work. Peter inevitably becomes morally corrupted and at
the end of the novel runs away to sea to escape the bitter antagonism of
the rest of his family whose lives he has betrayed.

The lot of the women in the novel is many times worse than that of the
men. Mrs Fury is worn out with waiting on the men in the household, including her very aged and senile father who from the beginning of the
novel up to the end is always found sitting in the kitchen, strapped to a
chair to avoid falling off; spoon-fed and speaking gibberish. The kitchen
in which the reader always finds Mrs Fury is described in great detail like
the dark interior of one of Gorky's peasant homes—a small altar with a
candle burning that has been alight for seventeen years, casting a dim
flickering light onto the features of the senile old man. At the end
Mrs Fury almost gives up eating in order to accelerate the process of her
own dying, a woman destroyed by class and sexual oppression. Her last

act in the novel is to attack Peter when she finds him about to board ship. She tries to pulp his face which stands for the face of all the men who 'had cheated and insulted her'.

2. George Garrett

By the mid 1930s Hanley was getting regularly published in those two important outlets for new writers, particularly those from working-class backgrounds: *Left Review* and John Lehmann's *New Writing*. This was also true of George Garrett. Garrett, like Hanley, was born at the turn of the century into a Liverpool-Irish Catholic family. He went to sea on leaving school, was back in Liverpool to join the 1922 Hunger March to London, went to sea again, travelled around the United States, joined the Wobblies, and finally returned to active working-class politics in Liverpool where he remained until his death in 1966. He had a number of stories published in *Left Review* and *New Writing* in 1935-37.

One such story, 'Redcap',[4] tells of a ship in a French port during the First World War. The sailors have been forbidden to go ashore and a military policeman stands on watch to ensure that this order is kept. The hatred of the sailors for this bullying and arrogant figure of authority, keeping them imprisoned on the ship for no real reason, is intense. An older sailor and a younger colleague manage to give the MP the slip one afternoon and get into town to buy some new boots and have a drink. They learn from some British rank-and-file soldiers in town how particularly vicious this MP is. On their return to the boat they are unluckily spotted by the guard who speaks to them with contempt and announces that they will be severely punished. The older man, a veteran of the Boer War and conscious of the way in which working-class people are pushed around in the services and in civilian life, edges the MP towards the wharf edge where he stumbles over a rope and falls into the water. Shouting for help, the MP struggles in the water trying to swim to safety. As if to help him the older man jumps into the water landing deliberately on the MPs head, stunning him and then allowing him to drown. It is a story of terrible frustration and hatred in which the ending, callous though it seems, also seems inevitable and just. Garrett, like Hanley, is concerned with extreme circumstances. Thus they write with vivid intensity of people whose consciousness is frequently at fever pitch. Psychological portraiture is of great importance to them.

Another story, 'Fishmeal',[5] shows Garrett at his most expressionist.

This is yet another examination of the terrors of the stoke-hold. In the sailor's quarters the men are grumbling about watch duties. Costain, very much an isolated figure, although ill decides to report for his next shift in the stoke-hold. At work in the heat of the stoking ovens he becomes feverish and mentally deranged. His mind is filled with fantasies of fire and thirst as his body is racked by fever. Suddenly he rushes from the stoke-hold up to the deck screaming and hurls himself into the freezing sea in order to assuage his physical thirst and mental turmoil. A small dinghy is lowered overboard to try to rescue Costain, but he is dead when they finally reach him. In the process of this rescue another sailor loses the use of both his arms as they are crushed while bringing the small boat back to the side of the larger ship. As the body of Costain is winched aboard, Garrett describes it as hanging like Christ at the Crucifixion. In both the stoke-hold and the wild night sea Garrett paints a picture of utter desolation and extremity.

In June 1936 Garrett also wrote (in *The Adelphi*) a particularly 'incisive' essay on Conrad's *Nigger of the Narcissus*. As an experienced seaman he was in a good position to take Conrad to task for a certain 'artistic' loading of the dice against the character Donkin—Conrad's miserable scapegoat at the centre of that famous story. Garrett brings to his criticism a very real understanding of the pressures and material circumstances which force Donkin into the role of an argumentative 'sea-lawyer' so despised by Conrad. At a number of key points in the story Garrett challenges Conrad's plausibility in the actual details of seafaring practice. Whereas Conrad invites the reader to identify with the Captain and the pride of the shipowners at the expense of the poorly fed, overworked and miserably paid seamen, Garrett in his critical essay suggests that the reader attempt for a change to identify with the sailors who actually do the work that creates the circumstances for Conrad to write his moral tale. Looked at in this new light, Conrad's selectivity of material appears artistically quite damaging. Conrad's final assessment of Donkin is thus: 'Donkin, who never did a decent day's work in his life, no doubt earns his living by discoursing with filthy eloquence upon the right of labour to live.' Garrett, on the other hand, supports the attitude and character of Donkin on the basis of real experience of the difficulties and tribulations of such a sailor's life. At the end of his essay Garrett looks forward to the day when, 'the Donkins might write the story of the sea. Let's hope it will be to better a world in which shipowners can still send out heavily insured coffin ships and their helpless crews.' It is salutary to be reminded that Conrad—much of whose reputation was based on the 'authenticity' of his seaboard settings—should be regarded as quite ignorant of many seafaring matters by sailors themselves. Garrett was not alone among these writers in being critical of Conrad. The narrator in one of Hanley's stories, 'Jacob', says that 'Conrad was not a sailor, but a writer who happened to go to sea.' If there was one fictional creation of sea-going life they all admired, then it was Big Yank, the hero of Eugene O'Neill's expressionist play, *The Hairy Ape*. Big Yank was the obsessed and frenetic stoker in extremis. Garrett's first performance as an actor was in O'Neill's play.

Garrett also wrote some autobiographical reminiscences and descriptions of important political movements in Liverpool in an unpublished work, 'Ten Years on the Parish', although the pieces on 'The First Hunger March' and *Liverpool 1921-22* were published separately. For some reason he seems to have given up writing at the end of the 1930s, an event which John Lehmann to write in the first volume of his autobiography, *The Whispering Gallery*, published in 1955: 'If George Garrett, Liverpool seaman and heroic battler against impossible odds, should by any chance read these works, I should like him to know how much I have always regretted that he found it impossible to go on with what he had so vigorously begun; and I should like him to tell me what happened to him.'[6]

3. Jim Phelan

As mentioned before, Garrett and Phelan knew each other and from time to time met when their very circuitous paths crossed. Phelan was born in a small village outside Dublin in 1895 and first ran away from home when he was three. He ran away from home for good around the age of eleven and settled for a while in Dublin, working as postboy and living in the anonymity of the slum area called 'The Liberties'. He quite soon decided to go to sea and eventually, like Garrett, tramped across the United States. In one of his stories, 'Happy Ending', the narrator describes the life of a man never at rest: working various passages as a sailor, occasionally meeting up with old friends on different ships, or on casual jobs like grape-picking in France, or living rough in seaports like Marseilles (a city which also fascinated Hanley and provided the setting for his novel *The Closed Harbour*). In his autobiography, *The Name's*

Phelan, Phelan writes of his lifelong obsession with flight: 'Always, in any danger of difficulty, my immediate impulse is to turn round and head for the horizon.' The chronology of Phelan's life is difficult to reconstruct since he never gave any dates in his autobiographical writings. We do know, however, that Phelan had been a member of the Irish Republican Army and was convicted in 1923 for the murder of a man in the course of a post office robbery in Liverpool. Condemned to death, he vividly describes in his autobiography the days he spent in Strangeways prison waiting to be hung. The death sentence was commuted at the last minute, but he remained in jail until 1937—a period which is the subject of many reminiscences in *Jail Journey* and *Tramp at Anchor*.

One novel, though, *Ten-A-Penny-People* (1938), perhaps his most sustained work, falls into place quite readily next to the themes and preoccupations of Garrett and Hanley. Published by Gollancz in 1938, it begins in Liverpool with a young boy about to be persuaded by his father to start work on the boats. The opening scene is very similar to those of Hanley's novels and equally powerful. Joe Jarrow (not a very careful disguising of the Joe Jarrett alias George Garrett of the later autobiography) is the young man who refuses his father's place as a trainee stoker on board a ship about to sail, takes on his father in physical combat, and after a brutal slugging match is finally beaten into unconsciousness. Standing over his supine son the father unbuttons his fly and 'watered the face of the unconscious boy'. Phelan is very much in the same horrendous territory as Hanley. The young boy is taken on board ship where he is immediately befriended by an older sailor known as 'Soshie' (the socialist) who gives him a volume of Jack London stories. The novel then quickly moves to a completely different setting with different characters which sets the structure for the rest of the book. For this is a discontinuous succession of scenes and plots, sometimes overlapping and related, sometimes not, as Phelan tries—for the most part successfully—to break away from the determinations of the continuous narrative to present a patchwork of parallel sequences which can be made to represent simultaneity of working-class life and struggle in various places at the same time. So Joe Jarrow turns up in the novel some years later in another sequence as a tramp.

It is likely that Phelan was very much influenced in his choice of style for this novel by the success of John Sommerfield's *May Day* published two years earlier in 1936. Sommerfield's novel itself owed much to the imagery and construction of the documentary film movement of the late

1920s and early 1930s—films like those of Eisenstein and Dovchenko with their dramatic crowd scenes, non-naturalistic lighting, images of individual anguish as well as processions, funerals, work in fields and factories, and villainous kulaks and capitalists. Novels like those of Sommerfield and Phelan owed even more to those documentary films whose aim was to capture the multi-faceted reality of city life, of which Ruttman's *Berlin: Symphony of A City* was the most seminal. When the British documentary film-maker John Grierson was describing the imagery of that particular genre of film, the 'symphony of the city', he could as well have been describing the techniques of the working-class expressionist writers like Sommerfield, Phelan, Hanley and Garrett: 'The day began with a processional of workers, the factories got under way, the streets filled: the city's forenoon became a hurly-burly of tangled pedestrians and street cars. There was a respite for food: a various respite with contrast of rich and poor. The city started work again, and a shower of rain in the afternoon became a considerable event. The city stopped work and, in futhermore hectic processional of pubs and cabarets and dancing legs and illuminated sky-signs, finished its day.'[7]

Phelan's *Ten-Penny-People* is built around a number of different incidents which happen at roughly the same time. The opening sections give the formative incidents in the early lives of some of the characters who assume much more important roles later on. Some chapters are prefaced by parts of folk songs or political songs, some by ironic Brechtian interventions. Other sections of the novel are simply snatches of 'representative' kinds of conversations, juxtaposing bits of talk around tea in a working-class household with voices of businessmen choosing from the menu in an expensive restaurant. There are central incidents which touch in different ways all of the characters' lives: a strike, a case of arson with murder at the same factory, a failed attempt at suicide by a woman which results in the death of one of her children and a murder charge against her. Some characters know about these things because they are directly involved, others only hear of them as news items.

In some ways Phelan is more successful than Sommerfield in creating believable characters, since Sommerfield as an active Communist was more concerned with creating representative 'types' of people who exemplified general psychologies of time and circumstance. Phelan, an anarchist by temperament and self-description, only dealt in generalities of character when he portrayed bosses or Party members. In fact there is a strong dislike in the novel for the politically rigid as in his portrayal of one Communist couple who can only ever speak in truncated phrases like modern Gradgrinds: ' "Interested", explained Dick. "Marvellous reflex-conditioning. Child knows factory really responsible. Works, poverty, tragedy. Marvellous reflexing. Agree?" he inquired, turning to Joan. "Agree", confirmed Joan. "Wages, want, woe-associated. Expressed as 'Poor Ma. The works.' Very striking." "Oh, go to hell, you cold-blooded pair of swine," shouted Kitty, as she dashed from the room.'

4. The Post-war Period

After the Second World War, Phelan mainly published books of autobiographical reminiscence, either about tramping or prison life, and occasionally short stories. Garrett, meanwhile, seems to have had nothing published after the war though he remained politically active in Liverpool. It was Hanley who carried on exploring the possibilities of fiction in a remarkably intense and prolific way. Among those with a very close interest in contemporary fiction, Hanley has become a writer who is from time to time described as 'the greatest living English language novelist'; yet outside such a circle of reviewers Hanley remains relatively unknown. This is a pity, for he has continued to take as the subjects of his novels the very real personal dilemmas of 'ordinary' people and treated these dilemmas and the lives which encompass them with an extraordinary sympathy and insight.

There are several reasons which may explain why Hanley's work has eluded popular attention. First, his novels usually take as their major preoccupation the psychological states of a very small number of characters locked in a very closed world of material circumstances. Little attention is ever paid to the wider society in which these characters live, although their lives are clearly deeply affected by social circumstances. Thus an early post-war novel, The Closed Harbour (1952), tells the story of a sea-captain, Marius, stranded with his wife and daughter in Marseilles, as he tries to get another engagement with a shipping company. We learn that something untoward happened on a previous voyage which makes his chances of another situation quite remote, but we never learn what really happened. The main emphasis of the novel is on exploring the obsessive desire of Marius to try to break free of the trap into which he has led himself and his family. His wife and grown daughter, both devout Catholics, regard him with increasing contempt as he wanders each day down to the harbour to try to secure another ship.

Marseilles is an overcrowded and corrupt city which breaks its inhabitants either on the wheel of a completely self-denying religion or through the 'corruption of the flesh' and desire for power.

The style of writing is very intense and highly metaphorical. Faulkner is an acknowledged mentor in Hanley's own development as a writer after 1945. Marius's mind begins to lose touch with reality as the realization that his life at sea has finished becomes confused with a metaphorical understanding of the decline of shipping. Looking at his old maps and charts, a sympathetic colleague tries to tell Marius that his experience already belongs to a past era, pointing to,'...the seas that had dried up, the ships that lay rotting, the rivers carrying nothing, the lighthouses without lights'. At the end Marius finds sanctuary in a hospital for the mentally ill run by a religious order, where everything is peaceful and quiet, but where, in such featureless and institutional surroundings, life had been 'levelled flat'.

Coming to terms with Hanley's style is not easy. Yet it has to be seen as a very conscious development from the novels and stories of the 1930s in which he usually set his characters in much more realistic, 'dynastic' and panoramic working-class settings. Some of his recent novels, published in the 1970s, exemplify both the strengths and weaknesses of Hanley's chosen style. *A Woman in the Sky* (1973) is a small masterpiece of expressionist stream-of-consiousness writing. It concerns a handful of characters living in a tower block on a North London housing estate, especially two elderly women who live together in one flat and their neighbours, an elderly couple next door. Such plot as there is, is precipitated by the suicide of one of the elderly women, a working-class alcoholic, deeply ashamed of having been caught and charged for a shoplifting offence. Hanley uses the incident to explore the inner lives of the remaining woman and her neighbours as they have to cope with this 'minor' tragedy. Much of the novel is in speech; either the internal speech of the characters as they shuffle from flat to pub or shopping parade, or between them as they talk about the incident. This speech is often very dense and highly elliptical, but it achieves insights and understandings of the lives that people are driven to negotiate under the pressures of class, material circumstances and emotional difficulty, which one just doesn't find in the contemporary realistic novel.

On the other hand, *A Dream Journey* (1976), about a couple living in London during the war, is tortuously long and much of the writing impenetrable. Hanley makes no concessions to conventional narrative structure and one gets the impression that he never rises from his desk from the first page of the novel until the concluding line. The energy in his writing is amazing but is sometimes defeated by a failure to make any concessions to the need of his readers for moments of recapitulation or ex-egisis. Most recently, *A Kingdom* (1978) is more simple and, though not as accomplished as *A Woman in the Sky*, remains a very powerful portrait of two sisters, long estranged, meeting on the death of their father. Again, these are not members of the kind of class which most modern fiction assumes to be the most important—the class to which most writers them-selves belong—but people (like Cadi and Lucy in this novel) who work in shops or look after elderly parents on smallholdings in Welsh villages. Hanley has said that he is fascinated by the supposedly 'inarticulate', whose inner minds are actually like 'great forests or endless seas'.

The Expressionist Mode Today

As there is once again a growing worker-writers movement in Bri-tain—which re-emerged significantly with the setting up of the Scotland Road Writers' Workshop in dockside Liverpool in 1972, demonstrating how resilient some apparently broken traditions can be—the achieve-ments of these three novelists are of more than academic interest. For they were writing in a period when experimentation in cultural forms often went hand in hand with revolutionary ideas in politics. Modernism was more than just an aesthetic movement, it also had political implica-tions. That connection has since the Cold War been completely broken: revolutionary politics has come to be associated with the most dull and unimaginative expectations of what is possible in literature, usually pedestrian verse and prose only distinguished from its 'bourgeois' counterparts by the worthiness of its morality.

Garrett, Hanley and Phelan did not try to develop a 'proletarian' aesthetic completely independent from the achievements of writers who had emerged—often antagonistically—from more bourgeois cultural traditions. Eclectic in their reading, they were excited and inspired by writers as various as Ibsen, Strindberg, Synge, Joyce, Gorky, O'Neill, Dostoesky, Faulkner, Jack London and Ben Traven. I believe they were right to think that a new literary aesthetic could not be developed without reference to the achievements of the bourgeois literary tradition which, if critically read and absorbed, could only provide a greater range of styles and techniques for exploring the multi-faceted and complex world of working-class experience. The material circumstances of their early lives as seamen and itinerants naturally influenced their choice of literary influences and iconography. The era of the great steel transatlantic passenger and cargo ships provided a number of political and experimental writers with the metaphorical images they needed: Ben Traven's *Death Ship*, Jack London's *Sea Wolf*, Conrad Aiken's *Blue Voyage*, Malcolm Lowry's *Ultramarine*, O'Neill's *The Hairy Ape* and the transatlantic voyage in Kafka's *America*. Before them, both Melville and Conrad had explored this world of harrowing sea voyages in equally allegorical ways. The Liverpool-Irish writers were fully steeped in this literary tradition. And they also, like many of the writers, together with Gorky, were acquainted with and fascinated by the extraordinary characters found in the most poverty-stricken districts of the world's major cities and sea-ports. In the various criminal underworlds, in the cafes and bars of the red-light districts, in the sailors' missions and dockside lodging-houses, they saw how many people had tried to find some form of escape or retreat or alternative way of life to that of the factory system. They did not necessarily like or condone what they saw, but they realized it had to be explored.

Since we live in a new era of cultural displacement and migration (both within and between countries) we shall have to find the appropriate literary forms and styles which can explore and reflect these shifts and changes in people's lives and their material circumstances. As 'de-industrialization' and the movement of capital disrupts settled industrial communities, we shall need to make the break from the traditional working-class novel with its emphasis on the continuity of the diurnal family life. Displacement, fragmentariness, cosmopolitanism, the life on the streets rather than in the homes, cultural multiplicity are likely to be the new conditions of experience for the next generation of working-class people. Significantly it has been the new Black writers and feminist writers who have responded more quickly to these changing material conditions and have tried to find new literary forms able to reflect and explore the complexities of the new 'structures of feeling' now emerging. Yet there is an expressionist tradition within working-class writing as I have attempted to show, and it is one that is worth re-connecting to and developing. Garrett, Hanley and Phelan really accomplished quite a lot in a matter of years with very little support or recognition. It is an appropriate time to rediscover them.

5

Out of the Ghetto: The Literature of London's Jewish East End

It is one of the paradoxes of writing—particularly for working-class people—that the act of trying to represent the culture and geographical community in which the writer has grown up and lived is the first step by which the writer is separated from that life almost irrevocably. At the same time as many people acquire their first typewriter, they also acquire their first suitcase. The two are often connected. They might also feel a pressure to remove themselves in order to write: to another district, perhaps or often another city, where a particular district is known to be a place for 'writing'—Grub Street, Bloomsbury, Soho, Hampstead—as if the air were more conducive to writing and varied from postal district to postal district, and thrived at least better in a capital city.

Jewish East London, between the 1890s and the beginning of the Second World War in 1939, has been sufficiently mythologized in show-business reminiscences, the ghosted autobiographies of dance-band leaders and boxers, as well as a number of very fine and detailed Communist Party memoirs, for it to be acknowledged that a quite singular and complex cultural milieu was created in that period whose richness and vitality is still almost tangible to this day. That culture certainly produced many writers, and I want to look at the work of three of them. Between them they produced over a dozen novels and collections of short stories between 1934 and 1945 whose starting points were almost exclusively situated in Jewish working-class life in London's East End. The three writers are Simon Blumenfield, Willy Goldman and Ashley Smith. All of their work has been long out of print, which is a great pity, since much of it provides a valuable corrective to subsequent romanticizations of that specific culture in that era, written as it was directly out of experience rather than recollected in maturity and restructured in the light of the meaning of the lives they later came to lead. For when people look back they often impose a meaning on the past to convince themselves that events took a natural direction, were ordained in some way and that things could not have happened in any other way. Those writing at the time gazed into a completely uncertain future in which at times they thought anything was possible and at other times thought that nothing was possible at all.

Right from the early days of settlement by Jewish immigrants in East London, at the end of the nineteenth century, the task of establishing the community's own religious and cultural institutions began. Synagogues were either built new, or adapted from existing buildings. The synagogue in Brick Lane was in earlier times a Huguenot church. Today it is a mosque. The political tradition so comprehensively described in Bill Fishman's *East End Jewish Radicals*, particularly the secular and anarchist clubs, were a direct influence on many young Jewish workers who through them came into contact not only with the world of ideas and opinions, but also with the worlds of music, literature, art and the theatre. The Workers' Friend Club opened in Jubilee Street on 3 February 1906 was the home of an enormous range of activities, as Fishman describes:

> Much of the cultural activity, initiated by Rocker, centred on the stage. Here, almost exclusively in the *mame loshen*, took place lectures, concerts, recitations, sketches (sometimes written by the performers themselves concerning current labour themes) and plays—classical and modern. Sam Goldenberg, erstwhile tailor turned star of the international Yiddish theatre, learned his stage-craft in the Club, where he was seen by 'Red' Rose performing as a young amateur in *Andreiev* and sketches of Sholem Aleichem. Here young Leftwich watched rehearsals of a Yiddish production of Ibsen's *Ghosts* and observed the making of the future maestro of Shakespearean theatre, Abraham Teitelbaum, on the same boards. Friday...was lecture night. Speakers would include Rocker, Tchekesov, Kaplan, Kropotkin, and Malatesta, on subjects ranging from world literature and science to modern political ideologies...'[2]

The Yiddish Theatre in Commercial Road was greatly frequented by young political activists and writers. Isaac Rosenberg was a regular theatre-goer before the First World War; the writers of the 1930s also reflected their familiarity with this theatre tradition in their short stories and novels. A third significant centre in the cultural life of Jewish East London was the Whitechapel Library where, under the supervision of a Mr Bogdin for more than forty years, young Jews came to read, talk and educate themselves. Both Rosenberg, the poet, and the painters Mark

Gertler and David Bomberg regularly used this library: Rosenberg autographed a copy of his early poems for Bogdin.[3] Another Whitechapel librarian, Morley Dainlow, introduced Rosenberg to the work of a number of Victorian poets—Tennyson, Browning and Swinburne, certainly—as well as writing comments on Rosenberg's own first attempts at poetry. Blumenfield, Goldman and Smith all mention the library at least once in their various fictional and autobiographical writings. The worker-poet, Julius Lipton, a tailor's presser, had his collection *Poems of Strife*[4] published in 1935 and noted in the frontispiece that the poems were 'Written in the Whitechapel Reference Library'. The important role this particular library played in many young Jewish workers' lives suggests one of those occasions when a state form—the public library in this case—can be 'won' by a combination of sympathetic staff and the users, and made into a popular cultural institution serving a particular community for its own purposes and in its own image. This is rare. For the history of state forms of provision, whether in health, education, housing, or culture, is for the most part the history of imposition and regulation. Elsewhere I have written of the important part played in the lives of working people by the institutions of the early working-class trade-union and socialist movement—in the history of Owenite halls, Chartist halls and schools, Co-operative centres and halls, working men's clubs and a plethora of small, often highly local initiatives organized by women and men for their own cultural and political purposes, including, of course, a scattered history of communes.[5] Once the labour movement embraced parliamentarianism that tradition of oppositional forms of self-organization and association was largely abandoned, though in the 1930s the Communist Party was admirably active in re-creating the tradition through such projects as the various Unity theatres, and more specific bodies such as the Workers' Film Movement, the Workers' Theatre Movement and its choirs, orchestras and other cultural networks.

In East London, though, a separate and active, self-contained and relatively autonomous culture of the Jewish working class existed as late as the 1930s, a kind of culture which had for the most part disappeared elsewhere, except for the mining villages of South Wales and parts of north-east England and Scotland—the 'Little Moscows' of Stuart MacIntyre's excellent study.[6] It is no coincidence that it is precisely these areas which produced such working-class writers who were able to find the time to write and the resources to get published in this same period. Thus Lewis Jones, Idries Davies and B.L. Coombes writing in South Wales;

Walter Allen, Leslie Halward and Walter Brierley as the 'Birmingham Group'; Garrett, Hanley and Phelan in Liverpool; Jack Lawson and Jack Common from Tyneside; Lewis Grassic Gibbon's trilogy, *A Scot's Quair*, covering the historical drift from land to city, Aberdeenshire to Glasgow, and so on. A strong sense of being outside conventional cultural patterns and routines not surprisingly characterizes these writers and their work. But in many ways the Jewish writers in East London were more prolific than the writers from other regional cultural formations, even though they were all writing about the one small district, whose intricacies of life and politics they never exhausted.

1. Simon Blumenfield

Simon Blumenfield's *Jew Boy* was the first of the autobiographical novels to appear from this group of writers and was published in 1935. The novel concerns two young East London working-class Jews, Alec and Dave, both in their early twenties, trying to make some choices about their futures out of the despair and hopelessness which they find around them. Alec inclines towards creating a distinctive Jewish socialist politics, whereas Dave is obsessed with sexual conquest and seems to spend his waking life pursuing this objective. One might well be the alter ego of the other. Alec's critique of the way in which radical Jewish culture is becoming diffused and fragmented is the most important motif of the novel and gives it some real weight as historical testimony. The old culture is losing its relevance. Alec and Dave still occasionally go to the Workers' Circle club in Alie Street (the building is still there) to listen to the Sunday concerts of Beethoven and Brahms, and mostly attended by an ageing generation of anarchists reading *Freiheit*. On the other hand, they see no serious future in the path represented by a number of younger Jews who are portrayed as trying to resurrect a rather anachronistic Jewish folk literature (presumably going back to the novelist Israel Zangwill as their mentor). At a party Alec has a book of poems thrust into his hand by the leading member of this school, called Leopold Hartmen in the novel and reacts thus:

> I glanced through his masterpiece 'Songs from the High Hills'. That was enough for me. There really isn't anything Jewish about Hartmen's work, or for that matter the work of almost any Jewish writer, writing in English. They're fakers, exhibitionists, poseurs, almost to a man. None of them

paints a truthful picture of the Jew as he really is. In England, at any rate, there aren't any more of their pet Jews left, with snotty beards, and greasy kaftans. Their characters are horribly sentimentalized: the 'Vich's', and 'Vots' and 'Schadchans' are laid on with trowels.

For Alec, class is as important as religion. Throughout the novel he is searching for an alternative way of life to that of the old culture, which is crumbling. He visits an old school friend who has moved out into the suburbs, and who now leads the life of the 'progressive' middle class. His bitter summary of the political ineffectiveness of this group—which must have made rather uncomfortable reading at the time, given the esteem with which this class formation regarded itself—is one of the most powerful sections of the book. Left on his own for a few minutes he surveys the bookshelves:

> Amongst others, Warwick Deeping, Ethel Mannin, David Garnett, Arthur Symons. Several Shakespeares...a Dickens set (probably from the Daily Mail) ...Bernard Shaw...H.G.Wells...Macaulay...Professors Lodge and Jeans...A fat Nuttall's dictionary...Fowler's Modern English Usage...
> Just what he might have expected. A catholic taste. Quite conventional middle-class, even to the ready-made guides to the Universe, handy keys to the problems of the eternal wheres and whyfores. A whole library of escape. You only had to pick up one of these books, and your mind soared into the vast empyrean, and you forgot there were such mundane things on earth as unemployment queues for example, and labour colonies, and filthy East End slums.

Alec meets a prostitute (who in many novels of the period under discussion are the only emotionally and economically independent women, particularly in working-class communities) and settles down with her. This is his most decisive break with his family and cultural tradition, to live with and possibly marry a *shiksa*, a non-Jewish woman. They get on well until the inevitable happens—an unwanted pregnancy—and this is terminated by an abortion that is as harrowing psychologically as it is physically. And here we come across a second key issue that characterizes many of the most influential novels of working-class life since the 1930s: the unwanted pregnancy and, in most cases, the subsequent illegal abortion. More than any other detail of working-class life, the illegal abortion is a kind of set-piece in such novels, marking the bitterest point of disillusionment and helplessness, much more so than any episode to do with work. The spectre of an unwanted pregnancy haunts the novels of

Blumenfeld and Goldman. Sillitoe's, *Saturday Night and Sunday Morning*, Bill Naughton's *Alfie*, Nell Dunn's *Up the Junction* and more recently Pat Barker's *Union Street* all make such traumatic abortions central incidents in their narratives. The main theme of Stan Barstow's novel, *A Kind of Loving*, was the ill-advised rush into marriage occasioned by the woman's pregnancy. And even though some of these writers were not themselves working class, it is significant that their portraits of working-class life naturally included this central fact of fear of pregnancy and the presence of the illegal abortionist in most working-class communities.

Alec is increasingly drawn into trade-union and left-wing politics, and the novel concludes with him vowing to dedicate his life to the cause of international working-class politics. The break is made from religion into politics. Alec finds his cultural identity in the struggle for socialism. Blumenfeld's *Jew Boy* (the title was clearly deliberately assertive) was, according to Joe Jacobs in his posthumously published memoir of East London Communist politics *Out of the Ghetto*[7] based on a rather singular Communist Party militant called Sam Berks, a widely known and admired figure in East London whose popularity was possibly connected with his ability to be fairly sanguine about party orthodoxy while remaining steadfastly active. 'I want Communism without Communists' was one of his most famous aphorisms.

In retrospect Blumenfeld's subsequent work seems to lack direction—the problem his main character worried about so much in his first novel. The next novel was a large-scale story of three generations, *Phineas Kahn: Portrait of an Immigrant*. The novel opens with the young Phineas in flight from the pogroms in Russia, first to Holland and then to London. He settles in Whitechapel, marries, fathers ten children, lives through various domestic tragedies and at the end of the novel returns to Russia, where his oldest daughter has gone to settle after the Revolution. It is a competently written novel, but with so many characters there is no real thematic development: it is simply the story of a large family and their tribulations. East London life only occasionally impinges on the lives of the characters.

Phineas Kahn was followed a year later by *Doctor of the Lost*, a fictional reconstruction of Dr Barnardo's life. Technically competent though it is, it fits strangely into a highly conventional and received tradition of seeing the East End working class as an abject and pitiful teeming mass, denizens of a nether world, who are only capable of being rescued from drunkenness and squalor by individual philanthropists and welfare agencies directed from without. Another year later *They Won't Let You Live* came. A rather programmatic left novel, it is built around a number of representative 'types', as in an updated morality play: the rich West End money-lender, the poor but honest working-class woman whom in earlier life he had got pregnant and abandoned, a Cockney taxi-driver who embodies all that is good and honest, a local fascist leader and a number of other part-players. Yet there are times when the novel really comes alive and grips the reader with the passion with which some of the scenes were clearly felt and re-created by the writer.

In *They Won't Let You Live*, Blumenfield reminds us of two particular kinds of pressure, one economic, the other cultural, which bit deeply into the community life of the Jewish East End and threatened many families with the real possibility of economic and social disintegration. The first was the plight of the small shopkeeper, insufficiently capitalized to survive in a vicious capitalist system of larger and larger chain stores and more intense credit squeezes. Today this plight may seem of little interest to those who would wholly base their definition of class on industrial, 'organized' workers, but it has to be remembered that in the Jewish East End political ideologies of socialism could, even had to, coexist with the world of small workshop production and small-scale family entrepreneurship. East London socialism, lacking for most of its history an industrial basis other than that of the dockworkers and their unions, and the clothing industry, has been more of an intellectual and cultural tradition, certainly within the Jewish community, a socialism fired by the very real oppression of material poverty and the anti-Semitism of populist right-wing politics. So, whereas in most other Labour strongholds you would expect shopkeepers and small businessmen to sit as Conservative councillors, in East London within my memory many such people have sat—and been effective—as left-wing Labour councillors.

In *They Won't Let You Live* two obviously sympathetic characters are driven to suicide as credit companies foreclose on them and force them into bankruptcy. Other lives are threatened by a different kind of insidious economic dissipation—that of gambling. There are moments of genuine tension in the novel as characters in financial extremes gamble what little they have left in the hope of being able to win back sufficient money to start repaying debts to corner shops, or to buy a roll of cloth that can be tailored into suits for another month's economic survival. The temptation, of course, in a world of small businesses was to 'borrow' money from the till for the last desperate gamble. The gambling underworld of bookmakers, street runners, billiard saloons, card schools in cafes, dog-track meetings was an ever-present abyss into which the Jewish male characters could fall. And in this novel Blumenfield reminds us of something very real and often very destructive within that culture which has tended to be forgotten. The worst thing that could happen in many Jewish families was for a son to slip into the gambling network and become a 'lowlife'.

Paradoxically, much of the ebullience and profligacy that people recall in the Jewish East End at this time reflects the inter-penetration, or co-existence at least, of underworld, political and aesthetic cultures. To be interested in writing did not necessarily mean that a young working-class Jew had to be uninterested in gambling, boxing, or, of course, radical politics. The best direct autobiographical account of the richness of this pre-war cultural milieu is that of Joe Jacobs in his account of his teenage years as a member of the Young Communist League in Stepney:

> I was getting to know more of East London as distinct from my East End. We were meeting dockers, seamen, municipal workers, builders, transport workers and so on, through the many TU and Labour organizations right through the area. This linked up with similar activities on an all-London scale. I was soaking up all I could read. It started with books like *The Ragged Trousered Philanthropists*, through to almost everything written by Upton Sinclair, Jack London, John Dos Passos, Romain Rolland, Mann, Remarque, Ibanez, Tolstoy, Gorky and so on. Then there came William Morris, Robert Owen, H.G. Wells, Arnold Bennett, J.B. Priestley. We got to know them all. Then there was the heavy stuff. It started with sections from Marx, published in pamphlet form—*Value, Price and Profit*; *Wage Labour and Capital*. There was the *Communist Manifesto*, great works I thought. Eventually, we went on to tackle *Capital* in full.[8]

It is interesting to note that English writers form very much a secondary list in the reading that he mentions—one thing that an internationalist political perspective engendered was an interest in writers from other countries. Jacobs then goes on to describe at length the Workers' Educational Association Classes at Toynbee Hall (where a post-war anti-fascist militant such as Alexander Hartog attended opera-singing classes that subsequently dominated his life[9]) with lecturers such as Brailsford, Laski and G.D.H. Cole; his interest in the Yiddish theatre in Whitechapel Road; in the British Workers' Sports Federation based at the Alie Street Workers' Circle Club; his following of the careers of the great Jewish boxers such as Ted Kid Lewis, Jack Kid Berg, Harry Mason and Al

Phillips; as well as his attendance at the local music halls—'The Paragon on the Mile End Road, as well as the Olympia and the London were my favourite haunts.' Who would dare to contest that this was a very abundant culture indeed? And it was not restricted to the Jewish community. Boxer-poets and docker-poets were also to be found in the non-Jewish community.[10]

In the course of all of these activities Jacobs met and courted a young woman called Pearl who, he found out, 'at one time was going steady with a chap called Willie Goldman who later wrote *East End My Cradle*. He had a friend, whose name escapes me, who fancied himself to be a poet. They seemed quite nice people and they all formed part of a wide circle of Young Communists who seemed to use the 'Circle House' as a base for their activities.'

2. Willie Goldman

It was Willie Goldman and his *East End My Cradle* which proved to be the most successful attempt to capture this extraordinary period in writing when it was actually happening. This autobiography had been fairly long in the making, and parts of it had already appeared as short 'documentary' stories in John Lehmann's *New Writing*. It is undisguised autobiography reconstructed with great passion and literary adroitness. In a short time it became the best well-known book about the Jewish East End and it remains the one that people still remember today, even among those who remember few others.

For the teenage Goldman family life was experienced as oppressive and restrictive:

> Parents here never have any problems about a son's future. It's all fixed at the cradle. There's only one small detail to think of: shall it be "ladies" work or 'gents'?'

The garment industry, or 'rag trade', was the major industry of East London, as it is today, though worked by a different generation of immigrant workers. Goldman's story is that of a young man who resists the pressures to conform to family and neighbourhood expectations, without really knowing what it is that he wants from life, like Alec in Blumenfield's *Jew Boy*. And so he recounts the different kinds of possibilities that presented themselves to him and his other male friends in their adolescent years.

The world of billiard halls and boxing clubs is one such possibility and Goldman evokes this—and the territorial and gang violence which they engendered—with a frightening realism. Subsequent accounts of this era have tended to gloss over the reality of Jewish involvement in the razor gangs, the race-track mobs and so on. This amnesia has had serious repercussions because subsequent generations of immigrants who have, not unsurprisingly, become involved in petty criminality for economic reasons have consequently been compared very unfavourably with what has become mythologized as a Jewish culture of unremitting hard work and complete respectability.

Similarly, adolescent sexuality and its frustrations are shown to be fairly traumatic; something that in retrospect most older people conveniently forget or gloss over with references to a 'higher standard of values' which young people allegedly abided by when they were young. In Goldman's account it was the common thing for young adolescent boys to be initiated into sexual activity by local elderly women, often the mothers of known school friends who could no longer ply as prostitutes in the West End or even compete in the East End pubs. In addition, of course, there were real infatuations that could be followed by strained courtships—often assiduously promoted by the families of the young people involved—pushing inexorably towards marriage and lifelong domesticity. *East End My Cradle* describes this more restricting side of Jewish East London well.

Yet the main theme of Goldman's first book, a theme that subsequently runs through all his later work, is the sense of becoming an outsider to the inherited family and neighbourhood culture, largely through the wish to become a writer. Of all the working-class writers of the 1930s and postwar years, Goldman is the most consistent explorer of this major cultural faultline: that between the working-class writer and the communal culture which becomes the subject of the writing. For though the writers might see themselves as chroniclers, folklorists or amanuenses, those written about could come to regard the writers as informers, collaborators and spies. Though this applied particularly to writers, it also applied to those who were not prepared to follow past traditions and wanted to make a future for themselves, independently. Apart from writing about himself in this respect, Goldman also writes at length about the tragedy of his school friend Wise, who he meets up with several years later in the Whitechapel Library reading room. By this time Wise is set on the idea of developing his talent as a painter, an ambition bitterly resented by his family. Goldman recounts:

> To his people he was a 'problem'—but not a psychological one. He was merely the problem of the 'no-good'. That was their explanation of his artistic ambitions. He was 'too big for his boots'. They felt he had no right to be 'different'. People with warped lives will forgive you anything but being different from themselves.

Wise manages to get into an art school but finds that he can't afford the fees, which his family refuse to pay. No support is forthcoming once he decides to break away from the family expectation that he should follow everybody else into the tailoring trade. So he becomes a drifter, sleeping rough or occasionally, in one of the 'Rowton Houses', rapidly deteriorating in health and mental well-being. Within a year of their meeting up again, Wise has died of 'Delirious Mania and Exhaustion' in Colney Hatch Asylum. It is the bitterest moment in Goldman's chronicle, and elicits the savagely critical, if finally rather rhetorical, judgement that, 'That is why my birthplace will always draw me at the same time that it saddens me; there, in that little graveyard of human hopes lie their murdered aspirations...'

Goldman goes on to talk about his own aspirations—to be a writer—and in his account of his own struggle to find both a form and style to match the political passion of his own sense of injustice, he raises issues that still have a relevance—how to make a literature out of what begins as politics. Even his own attempt, in these particular paragraphs, to describe the problem of avoiding over-writing and the too ready employment of clichés, exemplifies the problem:

> One night when sleep became difficult for the hunger gnawing in my stomach and the strange tumult in my head, I dressed and went out into the cold grey streets of East London's dockside. I saw the wretches huddled in doorways and ragged prostitutes slinking by walls, and I wept at their misery and my own. There arose in me at the same time the desire to scream the story of our common fate into the face of the world. It soon took me like a fever, and I tramped towards home with my hunger forgotten in the ecstasy of a new-found resolution.
>
> I sat down at my table and wrote without pause. I wrote what I had seen. It was not a story—it was a statement. Tears again flowed down my face as I re-lived the experience on paper, but they must have been tears engendered by self-pity, for when I re-read what I had written next day I was unable to recapture my original emotion...I was made miserable by the

futility involved in continually producing masterpieces at night that showed up as counterfeits in the morning.

East End My Cradle ends with Goldman beginning to earn small sums of
money for articles and receiving a favourable reader's comment on a
novel he had submitted to a London publisher. As a writer, he concludes,
he has made a start in life.

The next book of Goldman's to be published (unlike Blumenfield's
books, there seems to be no relationship in Goldman's work between
when books were written and the order in which they were published,
which makes reading them as a developing body of work impossible), *The
Light in the Dust*, which came out in 1944, is certainly not the novel mentioned in *East End My Cradle*. Instead it is a curious work claiming in the
introduction to be based on the diary of another young East End Jewish
writer who killed himself and whose papers and notes came into
Goldman's hands. Internal evidence suggests strongly that this was a
device, and that in fact the character is Goldman himself, whose own early life and political involvements are very much those recorded in the
'diary'. However, it is certainly true that a young would-be writer known
to Goldman killed himself at the time when it is claimed the diary was
written. This we learn from Maurice Levinson's autobiography, *The
Trouble With Yesterday* published in 1946.[11] Although not directly mentioning Goldman, Levinson talks about going to Communist Party
meetings with a Max and a Willy, and also spending time at the Whitechapel Library with the same pair. Willy is almost certainly Goldman
himself and Max may well have been Goldman's friend Wise, for in
Levinson's book Max dies young of malnutrition and poor health. But
Levinson mentions another young man whom he calls Stukey, a writer
known to them all, who killed himself at the age of twenty-two, which
would have been about 1933. So it is likely that Goldman based *The Light
in the Dust* on a real event.

The image of the writer in this period—very much in evidence in the
work of the East End writers—is that of a doomed Keatsian (male) hero,
innately talented, scorned by those around him and preordained to
sacrifice his health, and possibly sanity, in the quest to describe some
final Truth about life and experience. The pervasiveness of this received
idea, or specific cultural discourse, meant that in practice these young
writers did sit writing into the night in solitude, unsupported by the
solidarity of other writers and political friends, and that they saw their

project as one of producing a completely personal testimony, which had to be achieved in spite of other people rather than in common cause with them. Made to feel isolated because they wrote, they then isolated themselves further in the cause of writing, invoking the highly self-destructive notion of the probable necessity of starving in a garret. Here is the anonymous diarist writing about the effects of first getting published:

> I have recently had my first two short pieces published in a Socialist literary monthly. This fact has not changed my social or economic status in the least. In a certain sense it has even had an adverse effect on me socially; the family now suspects what I am up to. The Monthly is sold in a local bookshop, so others besides the family have discovered about my literary activities. The general notion, I gather, is that perhaps I am a queer guy, not like themselves, perhaps nasty even. 'If he's got brains, why not go in for something healthy and normal, like a crossword puzzle or picking winners?'

The writer goes on to recall a life, on leaving school, mostly spent at the Whitechapel Library reading room. He describes his unenthusiastic membership of 'the Party', with whose literary magazine he feels himself to be in total disagreement, and final months spent in the unsatisfying company of middle-class literati, drinking in pubs in the Leicester Square district. This last period was not incidental for it anticipated the general drift of East London writers to Charlotte Street and Soho after the war, which we shall see later had significant implications both for the writers and the 'community' they left behind. One last quote from this book seems to represent Goldman's literary aesthetic, which is worth recording:

> My position now is that though I am still preoccupied by what is called 'ordinary life' as a subject matter, I am against the bare recording reporting method which is considered its natural form. Such a method leaves unexpressed those valuable aspects of fantasy and lyricism which, for me, exist as an integral part of all life, no matter its 'ordinariness'. The edict that literature is 'life seen through a temperament' seems to me as a truth indestructible and permanent...[12]

Goldman's next published novel, *A Tent of Blue*, was the story of a marriage. Again, the opening sections had already appeared as stories some years before in Lehmann's *New Writing*. In the early part of the novel two young 'rag trade' workers, Lotte and Ben, meet and conduct a light-hearted courtship that results, inevitably, in Lotte's pregnancy.

This is well done. The wedding, which is hastily arranged by both families, is felt by the couple as on occasion more like a funeral, the beginning of a domesticity they didn't want to enter into so young, marking the end of a small era of personal freedom which had hardly begun. So Goldman makes the wedding ceremony and party a ghastly parody of a celebration in which everybody in turn weeps and laughs, dances and sings, whilst the couple themselves sit in the midst of all the gaiety, numb and frozen inside. The early months of marriage and the birth of the first child all happen within a relationship that is already routinized and emotionally dead.

By accident Ben becomes involved in a young Jewish theatre group, which meets in a room above the offices of the Bakers' Union, and in doing so he becomes involved with more politically and sexually independent Jews of his own age. Politics becomes his point of self-identity too. The novel ends with Ben's election as branch secretary of his union in the garment trade and in a mood of self-achievement he promises to try to make his marriage work. *A Tent of Blue* is rather broken-backed in that the first half, which deals with sexual and familial oppression, is well handled, whereas the second half becomes rather formulistic, and is in fact at odds with the psychological narrative of the first part.

In the same year that *A Tent of Blue* was published, Goldman also had another novel published, *Some Blind Hand*, a lifeless, geographically and culturally unlocated novel about a handful of young writers who agonize about their spiritual calling as such and spend their time hanging around the offices of publishers' agents and reviews editors, trying to pick up odds and ends of paid literary work. The novel seems to epitomize in one sense the crisis involved in the movement from a known and lived locality and culture, as the East End was for such writers as Goldman, to the cultural idiosyncrasy and amorphousness of Soho and Fitzrovia, a move that was made by many working-class writers in this period. *Some Blind Hand* is a novel describing how difficult it is to write a novel—always a sure sign that a writer has nothing left to say. Raymond Williams who, interestingly, himself had reason to be in and out of Soho in the late 1940s because he and Wolf Mankowitz had based their magazine *Politics and Letters* there described this cultural crisis when writing about the ethos of the literary magazines in that period, particularly Cyril Connolly's *Horizon*:

The peculiar tone of much thirties culture—descended from the Bloomsbury ethos—found its final expression in this magazine of the forties: above all, an extreme subjectivism, projecting personal difficulties of being a writer as central social problems.[13]

The same problem reappears in Goldman's next novel, *The Forgotten Word*, published in 1948. Its narrator, Harry, (who has, significantly, changed his name to the genteel 'Vincent' in the course of becoming a writer) lodges with a middle-class couple and spends most of his time pursuing sexual affairs in various parts of London and worrying about how difficult it is to be a writer. The notion of becoming a writer, by which the emphasis moves from the activity itself to some generic concept of the person who does the writing or (in the case of several of Goldman's main characters, doesn't) has by this time become one of the most disabling and enervating notions in the social relationships of cultural production. 'Vincent' readily accepts a commission to ghost-write the memoirs of an elderly doctor who would like his life's fund of amusing anecdotes recorded for posterity. Towards the end of the novel, once again in urgent need of money, Vincent writes to a sex-manual publisher offering his services as a copy-writer. The main thing, it seems, is still to be able to call oneself a writer. What is most tragic about this process is that it is almost certain that these last two novels were actually written during the war itself and the fact that Goldman could write two novels at this time without mentioning or bringing in the war, anti-fascist politics, the turmoils of the Blitz and wartime London, or any reference to the world-historical horrors of the Nazi occupation of Europe shows exactly how encompassing this trap was—that the cause of the ideology of subjectivism could blind you to the world.

Goldman published two more books at the beginning of the 1950s, a collection of short stories, *A Saint in the Making*, and another novel, *A Start in Life*. Both return to the world Goldman knew best and wrote best about—the Jewish East End. The short stories are often revised and re-written episodes from earlier books fashioned into more self-contained pieces. The novel is a serious portrait of a family and of how the son Yasha drifts away into the underworld and, once again, finds himself in the comradeship of socialist politics. One particular story in *A Saint in the Making* called 'There's heredity close behind me' is worth quoting because it returns to the problem of the suspicion with which the activity of writing was regarded by Goldman's family and neighbourhood. It's a short story about four brothers who have all come to assume a very real dislike of work, preferring whenever possible to 'loaf' as a way of life.

> We find we're rather proud of this. Especially as we've improved on my father's loafing by giving our own more subtlety. My brothers, who are in the clothing trade, unfortunately still have to do a great deal of work from time to time. But they claim, proudly, that I, who am a 'writer', have brought the family tradition of loafing to its logical conclusion.

It's the funniest sentence in the story and, of course, it is also the most bitter.

3. Ashley Smith

Ashley Smith's published work is very different from that of Blumenfield or Goldman. For although he, too, was a Jewish East Ender the characters in his short stories and novels are largely non-Jewish working-class people. His first book was a collection of short stories, *Children With Fire*, and was published in 1934 when he was only 26. The stories for the most part, though about working-class people, are written within an aesthetic and literary tradition which is not that of Blumenfield or Goldman. Rather he has adopted the aesthetics of the short stories of Joyce's *Dubliners* or Katherine Mansfield's *Bliss*, where the luminousness and momentariness of the atmosphere and mood created by the narrative is the most important part of the story. There is usually one character at the centre of each of these stories—a boxer who has failed to make the grade and is a has-been at 21, an elderly and now lonely social worker coming to the end of her career helping others, a young boy crippled in a street accident, a local beauty queen struck down by consumption—and they are mostly stories of hope extinguished by some arbitrary act of fate. The book was dedicated, as was common certainly for most first novels or collections of short stories by working-class writers in the 1930s, to a patron, Geoffrey West, who might well have been the same dedicatee as the G.W. of Maurice Levinson's *The Trouble With Yesterday*.

In 1937 Ashley Smith had his first novel published, *The Brimming Lake*, the story of a working-class family in which the husband is a rather impractical kind of socialist dreamer—a shopkeeper incidentally—who moves his family from the north-east of England to East London to start a new life after their shop fails. Although the main part of the story concerns the young son Terry's growth into adulthood and political and sexual awareness, Ashley Smith gives the subsidiary characters important episodes of their own so that the novel is more than just the story of a singular development. The author is also concerned with the disjunction between the failed shopkeeper Hegarty's political idealism and activity, and his simultaneous total disregard for his oppression of his own wife, Deirdre. The family begins to disintegrate towards the end of the novel as Hegarty drinks more heavily while Deirdre becomes obsessed with preventing her son Terry from marrying 'below himself'. Terry becomes resigned to settling down locally and blending into the life around him. The disintegration of the family is halted only by Deirdre's self-sacrifice when she deliberately becomes pregnant again and subsequently dies in childbirth, leaving Hegarty and Terry to build their world anew for the baby whose birth releases in them new energies and dreams.

You Forget So Quickly published in 1946 is a sequel. It deals with the effects of the Munich crisis of 1938 on a small group of office workers in East London, several of whom we have met before in *The Brimming Lake*. Technically the book is more formalist in that it incorporates some of the documentary techniques employed by other left novelists in the late 1930s, such as John Sommerfield's *May Day* and Jim Phelan's *Ten-A-Penny-People*. It is divided into seven chapters, one for each day of the week, and each day is the story of one of the characters with the others playing subsidiary roles on that day. (Pat Barker's recent *Union Street* employs the same technique.) The prospect of war looms like a black shadow over the characters' lives, and they all react differently. Some choose active opposition to the war, others adopt pacifism, some turn to jingoism and militarism, others to drink. The least likeable characters scheme to find a safe place in the Civil Defence bureaucracy. The book ends with news of Chamberlain's return from Munich and the office relaxes back into its old parochial optimism.

In between his first novel and its sequel in 1939, Ashley Smith had a book published called *A City Stirs*, an impressionistic account of twenty-four hours in the life of London, very much in the genre of the 'symphony of the city' which was developed in the 1930s. Elsewhere, I have tried to show how this literary genre was, I believe, developed by left-wing writers from the documentary film movement, particularly Ruttman's *Berlin: Symphony of a City*.[14] The aesthetic strategy of this genre was to show the multiplicity of experience in the life of the modern city, and by contrasting the lives of the rich and the poor to arouse a consciousness of contradiction and contrast. *A City Stirs* has no plot, is formally divided into twelve chapters beginning with 'Midnight' and ending with 'Late Night Final', and it reveals all of the difficulties of appropriating a form from one aesthetic mode (film) and using it for another (literature) without modification, or any other kind of mediation. The task of translating visual images into words is often difficult enough (these are often the bits readers skip), but when this is done for an unbroken length of one hundred and fifty pages communication breaks down completely. One paragraph gives some indication of just how dense such writing is and how inevitably self-defeating; even though the individual paragraphs have much merit and style:

> The controllers in power stations watch the rising chart as office lights are switched on for the charwomen to make their salutary rounds. In gas stations the levels fall as housewives cook their morning meals. In Threadneedle Street and Lombard Street baize-aproned caretakers are polishing brass name-plates. The conductor arms of trams are being swung, fizzling with electric sparks as they reach the wires overhead. The sleeping men on the cafe floors have disappeared like melting snow. The trains have carried the night workers to their odd day-time beds. Newsboys are beginning to call the morning papers. They run along with an air of bewilderment as they snatch at their creased sheets—as if they were conscious of a falsity, prophesying and informing so confidently at this early onset of a young day. The tide is not yet in, but they are telling the depth of the wave. The houses stand out in their sharpest silhouettes. The light is enough to show quite clearly the lines of their roofs and walls, but not strong enough to confuse the grey stones of its own brightness. Council roadmen are spreading sand on sloping roads, sweeping their heaped shovels with wide movements, as if they were scything grass. Belted busmen are hurrying to their depots, their ticket-punches in tin boxes under their arms.

Certainly there is movement here, and historical evocation, but to the contemporary reader it must have been hard work not made any easier by the conscious alliteration of the language and the prolixity of the detail. Reading it now, as a piece of documentary evocation, in small episodes, as one might read Mayhew's journalism, it's powerful and occasionally hypnotic. At the time it was probably considered a bold, but in the end unsuccessful, piece of technical experimentalism.

From the East End to Soho

We have noted, in Goldman's work, the drift at the end of the 1930s from East London to Soho. Since East London lacked any kind of infrastructure of cultural production, or organized networks of readers and other kinds of audience at that time, whether through a network of local venues for readings, pubs, or political and trade-union connections, that drift seems inevitable. Therefore the move was as symbolic culturally and politically as it was geographically. For not only did it involve a change of address, it also involved a change in aesthetics and literary ideology. The writers stopped writing about communities, or types of people, stopped trying to represent ways of living, cultural formations and class identities. Instead they started writing about eccentrics.

There had always been a link between Soho and the East End, because Soho also had a small but established Jewish community from the beginning of the century. As Chaim Lewis in *A Soho Address* wrote: 'Soho had its thriving ghetto in the spacious decades before the First World War. It was to some extent Whitechapel's overspill into the West End.'[15]

Chaim Lewis remembered at least five synagogues in Soho during his childhood and adolescence—he was born in 1911—and it even had a 'Christian Mission to the Jews'. Soho had been a centre of cosmopolitanism since the middle of the nineteenth century and was the first home of many political refugees and exiles. Marx lived there for a while and, as Stan Shipley demonstrated in his excellent *Club Life and Socialism in Mid-Victorian London*, the pubs, coffee houses and clubs in Soho sustained the link of radicalism between the O'Brienites of the Chartist era and the radicals and socialists of the 1870s and onwards.[16] In the 1930s it was the district which housed the thriving sheet music and record companies as well as film industry distributors. It was London's best-known red-light district and had thriving Chinese and Italian communities. Prior to the Second World War it was most often associated in people's minds with 'gangland'; after the war it became identified as a new Bohemia, London's answer to the Paris Left Bank or Manhattan's Greenwich Village. Every East End writer[17] made the journey there, even if only for a little while.

Ralph Finn was born in Aldgate, in a tenement block in the 'Tenterground' and became a journalist in Fleet Street. His first published book, *Down Oxford Street* (1940), was a series of cameos of the people to be found in Oxford Street during lunchtime at the scene of a street accident. Oxford Street, incidentally, marks the northern boundary of Soho. Finn is the only one of the East London writers to consistently portray British fascist character types in his writings. He was a prolific journalist who turned much of his journalism into books, and from 1944 onwards he had a regular column in *The People* under the title of 'Cameos'. Most of his writing was based around character sketches and flawed by a sentimentality and a readiness to draw too deeply from the well of pathos. In the 1960s he made his mark again after years of anonymity as a writer with two books of East London reminiscences, *No Tears in Aldgate* (1963), followed by *Spring in Aldgate* (1968). Both are valuable as historical testimony but both are also flawed by a terrible sentimentalism and retrospective moralism.

Roland Camberton was born in Hackney, probably around 1918 going by the evidence of his autobiographical novel *Rain on the Pavements*, which was published in 1951. This is a highly readable account of growing up in a Jewish family in a slightly more prosperous area than Stepney, though only a couple of miles north of it. What is significant is how Camberton's main character David, and his friends, once they begin to write poetry at school and at home, decide they have to spend their time in an appropriate setting. And so, from about the age of fourteen, they walk to Soho every Saturday and Sunday to sit in the coffee bars and soak up the authentic atmosphere 'in the wholly fascinating land of Soho'. The Soho they are talking about is pre-war Soho, but the setting for Camberton's novel *Scamp* published a year earlier is in fact Soho just after the war.

In many ways *Scamp* is the archetypal novel of the problem of the deracinated writer and has much in common with Goldman's later novels about the same theme. It is the story of a young writer, Ginsberg, who with another would-be writer, Bellinger, lives in a room in an apartment block in Bloomsbury 'collecting rejection slips'. The parallels with Gissing's *New Grub Street* are quite evident. For Ginsberg, 'a story a day, that was his minimum task; two thousand words, preferably with a plot, development, a climax and a twist. After six months of this routine, he was beginning to feel an intense hatred of the short story, in fact, of all writing.'

Scamp ends when Ginsberg has been able to inveigle money out of a widow he is privately coaching to start his own literary magazine. The woman gives him the money because it is of some importance and status for her to be able to know a real 'writer'. The aura of being a 'writer' is what keeps Ginsberg and Bellinger alive—for their writing certainly doesn't and probably couldn't. The Soho Camberton portrays is peopled by alcoholics, eccentrics, refugees and would-be novelists. There is no sense of a world beyond Soho, or of a country living through a period of economic and social reconstruction and of bitter post-war austerity. The only important problems are inside the writer's head.

Possibly the best-known East London Jewish writer after the war was Wolf Mankowitz. Alone of all these writers he went to university, Cambridge in fact, and there met Raymond Williams with whom he set up the journal *Politics and Letters* in 1947, with an office in, of all places, Soho. The journal only lasted a year but Mankowitz stayed on in Soho and began writing short stories and plays about East London Jewish life, which, for some reason, captured the popular reading public in unexpected ways. 'A Kid for Two Farthings', a moralistic fable about a young boy who befriends a goat which he believes to be a unicorn, set in the East End, and published in 1953 was soon made into a major feature film with a full star cast. This happened to another short story, 'Make Me An Offer', originally published in 1952, which was again made into a full length feature film. In a way they were ideal stories for a population living through austerity, and for Londoners in particular, many of whom had been uprooted and were living very much a day-to-day existence. For they were about dreams and luck. They were flights of fancy in which an innocent boy's fantasy affects the lives of all those around him and gilds their lives too, inspiring optimism and the importance of making the best out of what you have. They were about finding a priceless vase in a junk shop, or in the groundman's cottage rather than in the manor house. The Soho stories were about small ironies of fate and changes in fortune in the lives of the 'characters' who lived and worked in Soho. Mankowitz's collection, *Blue Arabian Nights*, which gathered together the stories he wrote while living in Soho between the mid 1950s and the mid-1960s are introduced as being about a time when 'London was still a suitable Samarkand for a self-made inventor of the long tradition of tellers of a thousand and one curious tales.'

Such stories were also to be found in various versions in the London evening newspapers at the time, stories 'Out of Court', character sketches of small criminals, or stories from the race-track or the dog-track. This was a period which was fascinated by the 'spiv' and the sad lives of small-time criminals, street traders and eccentric women vagrants; the mood for literature went through a second Dickensian era. Soho was also the home of the 'Pop music industry', which sprang up in response to the wave of excitement at the new American rock'n'roll music. The 2 I's cafe in Old Compton Street launched Britain's first home-grown rock'n'roll singer, Tommy Steele, and Wolf Mankowitz wrote a story about it that became a film starring Britain's second rock'n'roll idol, Cliff Richard. The roots of 'Swinging London' in the 1960s lay in the journalistic and literary cultivation of Soho in the 1940s and 1950s.

The most serious and reflective account of this move from working-class Jewish East London to the cosmopolitan, shifting world of Soho is Bernard Kops's *The World Is A Wedding*. One of the most important post-war English autobiographies, it is a portrait of the pressures and dislocations that marked English youth and popular culture after the break-up of the war-time, national cultural settlement. Published in 1963, by which time Kops was known as a poet and dramatist, it is primarily an account of the mental breakdown that follows a long estrangement from his family, who are still living in the East End, and an account of an anomic life as a Soho cafe-dweller and drug-user. In the Swiss Cafe in Soho he found 'a real sense of security for the first time in years. The characters accepted me just as I was.' He was then, like many others, drifting round with 'my manuscripts in a carrier bag'. One of the rare sources of income in that area was to be got by the buying and selling of second-hand books. Often the first step in capital accumulation in this daily trade was to steal a book from Foyles, which would then be sold for enough money to buy half a dozen second-hand books, which could then be sold separately for enough to get drunk with and eat a cafe meal. At the end of his narrative Kops has become a second-hand book-dealer with a stall just off the Charing Cross Road and reconciled with the members of his family who remain after his mother's death. It is much the best account of Soho in the late 1940s and of its bohemian underworld, though it's a rather glamorous way of describing what was a very rootless and self-destructive culture. Kops admits, too, that his early interest in writing was awakened by his hours of browsing and reading in the Whitechapel Library.

Colin Wilson's *Adrift in Soho* (1961)[18], though written in the third person and not from the standpoint of a Jewish novelist, provides much detail of the Soho of the late 1950s. Wilson's narrator, existentialist and would-be novelist Harry Preston, arrives in Soho because of its proximity to the major publishing houses. He quickly learns how dependent so many Soho habitués are on the rapid circulation of money in the second-hand and specialist book trade and also learns that nearly everybody he meets is 'writing a book'. Such an environment was, of course, exactly the last place to encourage writing because in such company it was always much more interesting to talk about the books you wanted to write than actually get down to write them. Julian MacLaren-Ross's *Memoirs of the*

Forties recounts much the same story for the more well-known and established writers who inhabited the Charlotte Street district north of Soho in
the same period and whose commitment to writing was dissipated in the
endless pub crawls and literary gossip, as was MacLaren-Ross's
himself.[19]

There are three more writers we must briefly mention who also addressed
at least part of their work to the theme of Jewish life and culture in East
London in the 1930s: Arnold Wesker, Alexander Baron and Emanuel
Litvinoff. Wesker's trilogy of plays, *Chicken Soup with Barley* (1958),
Roots (1959), and *I'm Talking About Jerusalem* (1960), followed the same
family from the Communist and anti-fascist certainties of the 1930s to the
cultural dislocations of the 1950s and the geographical moves to
Hackney, and farther still to the middle-class suburbs of north-west London. The trilogy made one of the most stunning contributions to post-war
theatre history and accurately and sensitively portrayed what seemed to
be the ineluctable break-up of what had been, prior to the Second World
War, a tightly bound community that combined strong familial patterns
and connections with a fairly popular loyalty to Communist politics. As
material circumstances changed, and partly in the light of the Twentieth
Soviet Party Congress in 1956 which opened up the extent of the excesses
under Stalin, these political ties weakened, and in the move out of East
London political allegiances changed also.[20]

Alexander Baron grew up in Hackney, outside the classical 'East End'
where Jewish radicalism was at its strongest, and his development as a
writer took a quite different direction. Though active in anti-fascist and
Labour youth politics in the 1930s (and with a strong emotional involvement with the cause of the Spanish Republic from 1936 onwards), the
major experience that dominated his first novels was that of service life
during the Second World War.[21] His understanding of East London
politics in the 1930s qualifies the picture which has been passed on in
popular mythology in a number of important ways, and in the work of
other writers and playwrights. For the radicalism and internationalism
that marked much Jewish politics in this period was not necessarily
shared by the East End working class in general. The great popular
political 'moment' of the Battle of Cable Street in 1936, when many
trade-union and working-class socialists joined with the Jewish community to prevent the British Union of Fascists marching through East London, has tended to obscure other real political allegiances in the East End
at the time. For while many non-Jewish working-class people in East

London were loyal to 'Labour' politics, many were attracted by the class politics of fascism.[22]

Baron's version of the East London 'Jewish novel' was *Lowlife*, published in 1963 and, in my opinion, one of the best. It is a post-war portrait of a middle-aged man, living on his own in a small flat near Stamford Hill, a strongly Jewish district just outside the East End, whose waking life is divided between reading and gambling. It is a detailed study of a 'type' who is only obliquely referred to in most other novels of Jewish East London. Its main character, Harry Boas, has broken most family connections and lives out a self-sufficient life half-way between the old world of the proper 'East End' and the new world of the suburbs. There is also a very moving secondary motif that weaves in and out of the main story, concerning a youthful affair in Paris, the fathering of an illegitimate child and the disappearance of that child and its mother on one of the sealed trains to Auschwitz or Buchenwald. This simple story provides a very accomplished and moving novel. *With Hope, Farewell* (1952) is primarily a story about a young Jewish man who becomes a pilot during the war but the opening and closing sections are set in East London, in the late 1920s and the post-war 1940s, and these are very atmospheric in capturing both time and place. *The In-Between Time* (1971) is about the Labour League of Youth politics in Hackney during the 1930s and the attempt to get to Spain to fight for the Republican cause. Baron's free-thinking Jewish background, and the fact that he grew up outside Jewish East London proper, clearly freed him from the pervasive intensity of that world as described in the writings of Blumenfield and Goldman, and gave him more fictional distance.

The most recently published book evoking that pre-war world is Emanuel Litvinoff's *Journey Through A Small Planet* published in 1972 and written in the form of fully shaped short stories told chronologically. They are very funny, and most of the humour is that of self-deprecation as the narrator sets his own political seriousness and dreams of revolution against the realities of his everyday struggle in life. It is wonderful writing, but its political and aesthetic impulses are those of evocation and nostalgia. For by the time such writers as Ralph Finn and Emanuel Litvinoff decided to set down their accounts of the Jewish East End, they were leading lives in complete contrast to the world they evoked. For them, that quite singular and enormously fertile culture had become, to a large extent, simply the material for a different kind of brilliant and gem-like writing. And the readers who would have recognized their early lives in these books were mostly already in exile themselves. Literature came too late to save politics. The connections had all been broken. The castle had been abandoned.

Books Mentioned in Chapter 3

Fair Stood the Wind for France, H.E. Bates, London 1958
From the City, From the Plough, Alexander Baron, London 1948
There's No Home, Alexander Baron, London 1950
With Hope, Farewell, Alexander Bacon, London 1952
The Human Kind, Alexander Bacon, London 1953
The Cage, Dan Billany with David Dowie, London 1949
The Trap, Dan Billany, London 1950
Escape or Die, Paul Brickhill, London 1952
The Dungeon Democracy, Christopher Burney, London 1945; *Solitary Confinement*, London 1952
Enemy Coast Ahead, Guy Gibson, London 1961
The Last Enemy, Richard Hillary, London 1942
Pebbles From My Skull, Stuart Hood, London 1963
Partisan, MacGregor Urquhart, London 1958
They Have Their Exits, Airey Neave, London 1953
Odette: Story of a British Agent, Jerrard Tickell, London 1956
Dispersal Point, John Pudney, London 1942
Flight to Arras, Saint-Exupery, 1943
Wind, Sand and Stars, Saint-Exupery, 1941
The Aerodrome, Rex Warner, London 1942

Books Mentioned in Chapter 5

Simon Blumenfield
Jew Boy, London 1935
Phineas Kahn, London 1937
Doctor of the Lost, London 1938
They Won't Let You Live, London 1939
Willy Goldman
East End My Cradle, London 1940
The Light in the Dust, London 1944
A Tent of Blue, London 1946
Some Blind Hand, London 1946
The Forgotten Word, London 1948
A Saint in the Making, London 1951
A Start in Life, London 1947
Ashley Smith
Children With Fire, London 1934
The Brimming Lake, London 1937
You Forget So Quickly, London 1946
A City Stirs, London 1939
Ralph Finn
Down Oxford Street, London 1940
No Tears in Aldgate, London 1963
Spring in Aldgate, London 1968
Ronald Camberton
Rain on the Pavements, London 1951
Scamp, London 1950
Wolf Mankowitz
A Kid for Two Farthings, London 1953
The Penguin Wolf Mankowitz, London 1967
Bernard Kops
The World is a Wedding, London 1963
Arnold Wesker
The Wesker Trilogy, London 1964
Alexander Baron
With Hope, Farewell, London 1952
The In-Between Time, London 1971
The Lowlife, London 1963
Emanuel Litvinoff
Journey Through a Small Planet, London 1972

Notes

Introduction

[1] *Raids and Reconstructions*, Hans Magnus Enzensberger, London 1976.

1 Fictional Politics: Traditions and Trajectories.

[1] Lennard J. Davis, *Factual Fictions: the Origins of the English Novel*, New York 1983, p. 125.

[2] Ibid., p. 97.

[3] Ian Watt, *The Rise of the Novel*, London 1963, p. 205.

[4] A. E. Dobbs, *Education and Social Movements*, London 1919, p. 101.

[5] Thomas Jones, *Rhymney Memories*, Wales 1970.

[6] Watt, p. 45.

[7] Davis, p. 103.

[8] Richard D. Altick, *The English Common Reader*, Chicago 1957, p. 24.

[9] Robert Escarpit, *The Book Revolution*, London 1966, p. 23.

[10] Altick, p. 99.

[11] P.M. Ashraf, *Introduction to Working-Class Literature in Great Britain*, Volume 2, Berlin (GDR) 1980, p. 13. This volume together with its companion volume on poetry constitutes one of the most thorough histories of working-class literature in Britain in the 18th, 19th and early part of the 20th centuries. It is, shamefully, unpublished in Britain.

[12] *Respectable Radical: George Howell and Victorian Working-Class Politics*, London 1971.

[13] Ibid., p. 13.

[14] Altick, p. 133.

[15] In for example Altick, *English Common Reader*; Louis James, *Fiction for the Working Man*, London 1973; Victor Neuberg, *Popular Literature*, London 1977; Brian Simons, *Education and the Labour Movement*, London 1960 and 1965; R.K. Webb, *The British Working-Class Reader*, London 1955 and W. Wickwar, *The Struggle for the Freedom of the Press*, London 1928.

[16] Neuberg, p. 113.

[17] Harry McShane and Joan Smith, *No Mean Fighter*, London 1977.

[18] Ashraf, *Introduction to Working Class Literature*.

[19] The novels are too numerous to mention. In the past ten years a number of feminist publishing houses have been started in Britain, including Virago, The Womens' Press, Onlywomen Press, Sheba Press and others.

[20] See Claud Cockburn, *Bestseller*, London 1972.

²¹This possibly contentious thesis remains an intuition. I stand by it, for all that. In my own experience, an active involvement in the Labour Party Young Socialists in a provincial town in the late 1950s and early 1960s also meant the circulation of books among a group of young people by such writers as Camus, Sartre, Kerouac, Mailer and Miller, the City Lights of the Beat poets, and so on. All of this was going on well outside the sphere of influence of the universities or the London literary magazines. The youth culture that formed the milieu for these reading patterns was an increasingly politicized one. This is also the impression given by Jeff Nuttall's *Bomb Culture*, (London 1970) though he seems to me to dwell too narrowly on the London scene and the influence of the Art Colleges. Such American writers as Salinger, Bradbury and Kurt Vonnegut were read first within the orbit of popular youth culture, then as class books in English secondary schools and only later as part of the university English programme. Far from being in the vanguard of literary developments, the universities lag far behind the interests and concerns of oppositional cultures, such as the various youth cultures, and the feminist movement.

Clearly the existence of Penguin books was of real material importance in encouraging the interest of young people in European and American writing in the 1960s. In their classic study of the working-class grammar school pupil, *Education and the Working Class*, Brian Jackson and Dennis Marsden noted how many of the people they interviewed had much of their reading almost 'directed' by whatever Penguin published.

²²John Field, *The Archetypal Proletarian as Author: the Literature of the British Coalfields 1919-1939*, Northern College 1981.

²³See Dave Morley and Ken Worpole, eds., *The Republic of Letters*, London 1982 for a partisan account of this movement. See also Jane Mace, *Working With Words*, London 1981.

²⁴Walter Benjamin, *One-Way Street*, London 1979, p. 45.

²⁵Peter Widdowson, ed., *Re-Reading English*, London 1982.

²⁶Escarpit, *The Book Revolution*, p. 34.

²⁷In the *Sunday Times*, of 5 June 1983 there was an account of a new series of ten historical novels of which all the plots were devised by a literary agent who then commissioned writers to provide the texts.

²⁸See Ken Worpole, 'Alternative Publishing', *New Society* 3 June 1979.

2 The American Connection: The Masculine Style in Popular Fiction

¹'Expressionism and Working-Class Fiction', originally published in *NLR 130* (November-December 1981).

²Thus this essay stands in total opposition to the 'socialist' criticism of popular literary genres adumbrated with admirable frankness by David Holbrook in his review of 'The Popular Arts' by Stuart Hall and Paddy Whannel in 1965 (*The Use of English*, XVII, 3, shows by his ironic asides that he knows what he is doing. I see no value in such 'discriminations': if we are to have muck, let's have outright, sheer muck rather than muck that pretends, by snobbery or irony, to be superior.' (p. 195).

³From a selection of Gramsci's writings on popular literature circulated by Tony Davies at the Birmingham Centre for Contemporary Cultural Studies.

⁴See Julian Symons, *Bloody Murder: From the Detective Story to the Crime Novel*, Harmondsworth 1974.

⁵*One-Way Street and Other Writings*, New Left Books, London 1974, p. 49.

⁶'Morelli, Freud and Sherlock Holmes: Clues and the Scientific Method', *History Workshop Journal* 9 (1980).

⁷*Bestseller: The Books That Everyone Read 1900-1939*, London 1972.

⁸Ibid.

[9]Colin Watson, *Crime Writers*, London 1978, p. 61.

[10]In *Essays, Journalism and Letters*, Vol. One, Harmondsworth 1970, p. 275.

[11]John Sutherland, *Fiction and the Fiction Industry*, London 1978, p. 3.

[12]See Renê Wellek and Austin Warren, *Theory of Literature*, Harmondsworth 1973, p. 235.

[13]From the BBC programme notes for the series *Crime Writers* (1978).

[14]See W. M. Frohock, *The Novel of Violence in America*, New York 1950.

[15]See D. Madden ed., *Tough-Guy Writers of the Thirties*, New York 1968.

[16]Sutherland, p. 22.

[17]Richard Hayman, *Shadow Man: The Life of Dashiell Hammett*, London 1981.

[18]Dennis Pepper ed., *A Hemingway Selection*, London 1977, p. 195. This anthology, which includes early reviews of Hemingway's work along with most of his well-known short stories, is, significantly, an edition for schools, and reminds us of how important American writing—Hemingway, Steinbeck, Salinger and so on—has been in the curriculum of British schools as a source of vivid narrative writing free of the class sentiment which distinguishes English writers of the same period. The accessibility and inventiveness of American writing continues to find a popular readership in Britain, where native writers conspicuously fail. In my own experience in teaching over the past fifteen years, the contemporary American writers who seem to be the most influential among young people in Britain are Ray Bradbury and Kurt Vonnegut, Junior.

[19]D. Gardiner and K. Sorley Walker eds, *Raymond Chandler Speaking*, London 1962.

[20]From *A Hemingway Selection*, p. 183.

[21]Ibid, p. 184.

[22]*The Art of Writing*, London 1916, p. 23. Yet in this period, significantly, Dorothy Richardson was, in the words of Virginia Woolf, developing something she consciously described as a 'women's sentence'. Gillian Hanscombe's recent study of Richardson (*The Art of Life*, London 1983) makes this question of a feminist style of writing a central theme and quotes Virginia Woolf's taxonomy of what such a syntax involves: 'a sentence of a more elastic fibre than the old, capable of stretching to the extreme, of suspending the frailest particles, of enveloping the vaguest shapes' (p. 40). Syntactic structures, then, are not merely questions of aesthetics but of class and gender as well.

[23]L. W. Wagner ed. *Ernest Hemingway: Five Decades of Criticism*, Ann Arbor 1974, p. 14.

[24]Frank MacShane, *The Life of Raymond Chandler*, London 1976, p. 48.

[25]Ibid, p. 81.

[26]London 1931, p. 105.

[27]Ibid.

[28]In Miriam Cross ed., *The World of Raymond Chandler*, London 1972.

[29]*Raymond Chandler Speaking*, p. 70.

[30]Jacques Barzun and W. H. Taylor, *Catalogue of Crime*, New York 1971.

[31]*Soviet Writers Congress 1934*, London 1977, p. 90.

[32]MacShane, p. 261.

3 The Popular Literature of the Second World War

[1]Boris Ford ed. *The Pelican Guide to English Literature: The Modern Age*, Harmondsworth 1961.

[2]Robert Hewison, *Under Seige: Literary Life in London 1939-45*, London 1979.

[3]Walter Allen, *Tradition and Dream*, Harmondsworth 1965.

[4]Ronald Blythe, *Components of the Scene*, Harmondsworth 1966.

[5]Stuart Hood, *Pebbles From My Skull*, London 1963, p. 153.

[6]Paul Brickhill, *Escape or Die*, London 1954, p. 10.

[7]M.R.D. Foot, *Resistance*, London 1978, p. 13.

[8]Ibid., p. 316.

[9]Ibid., p. 320.

[10]John Sutherland, *Best-sellers; Popular Fiction of the 1970s*, London 1981, p. 96.

[11]From a personal interview with Alexander Baron.

[12]Dan, Billany, *The Trap*, London 1950, pp. 23, 50.

[13]Ibid., p. 234.

4   Expressionism and Working-Class Fiction

*The catalyst for this essay was coming across a reprint of George Garrett's account of the Liverpool unemployment demonstrations in 1921-22. Reading this pamphlet, which contained an excellent bibliography of all Garrett's writings, also made me connect Phelan with Hanley in a way I hadn't before. The Garrett pamphlet, produced by Alan O'Toole in Liverpool, is a good example of how much we need these local studies before we can begin to make the more general connections of movements and ideas.

[1]*Illuminations* London 1970, pp. 84-85. In this essay Benjamin also makes some highly pertinent comments about the decreasing value attributed to the category of personal 'experience' by modernizing social systems and ideologies.

[2]See Raphael Samuel ed., *People's History and Socialist Theory*, particularly the section on 'Local History'.

[3]*The Name's Phelan*, London 1948, p. 276.

[4]*Left Review*, October 1935.

[5]*New Writing*, Autumn 1936.

[6]John Lehmann *The Whispering Gallery*, London 1955.

[7]*Grierson on Documentary*, London 1979, pp. 39-40.

5   Out of the Ghetto: the Literature of London's Jewish East End

[1]William Fishman, *East End Jewish Radicals 1875-1914*, London, 1975.

[2]Ibid., p. 265.

[3]Jean Liddiard, *Isaac Rosenberg: The Half-Used Life*, London 1975, has a whole chapter on the Whitechapel Library. See also A.B.Levy, *East End Story*, London 1951.

[4]Julius Lipton, *Poems of Strife*, London 1936.

[5]Ken Worpole, 'Buildings and socialism', in *The Leveller*, February 1978.

[6]Stuart Macintyre, *Little Moscows: Communism and Working-Class Militancy in Inter-War Britain*, London 1980.

[7]Joe Jacobs, *Out of the Ghetto*, London 1978.

[8]Ibid., p. 38.

[9]Alexander Hartog, *Born to Sing*, London 1978.

[10]Among the most well known are Jack Dash, unofficial dockers' leader for many years, whose autobiography *Good Morning Brothers!* was published in 1969, and Stephen Hicks, boxer and poet, whose autobiography, *Sparring For Luck* was published this year. A good anthology which represents this tradition is *Bricklight: Poems from the Labour Movement in East London*, (Chris Searle ed., London 1980) though it does tend to give the impression that working-class life, politics and culture is a recognizable tradition of unbroken continuity, an impression that I personally have serious reservations about.

[11]Maurice Levinson, *The Trouble With Yesterday*, London 1946.

[12]I've recently discovered that the definition of literature as 'life seen through a temperament' is J.B.Priestley's and comes from his introduction to George Douglas's highly influential *The House with Green Shutters*, an extraordinary novel now sadly neglected.

[13]Raymond Williams, *Politics and Letters*, London 1979, p. 72.

[14]See chapter 4.

[15]Chaim Lewis, *A Soho Address* London 1965.

[16]Stan Shipley, *Club Life and Socialism in Mid-Victorian London*, London 1972.

[17]Mark Benney's *Lowlife* (London 1936) is a classic Soho criminal autobiography.

[18]Colin Wilson, *Adrift in Soho*, London 1961.

[19]Julian MacLaren-Ross, *Memories of the Forties,* London 1969.

[20]A recent study, Geoffrey Alderman's *The Jewish Community in British Politics*, (Oxford 1983), has shown that with increased social mobility the Jewish vote has become more and more conservative.

[21]These novels are examined more closely in chapter 3.

[22]In a personal interview with me Alexander Baron said that '...in the East End of London the real mass politics was fascism and it became a real movement of the people for a period until it all melted away in those great rent strikes.' See also Phil Piratin's *Our Flag Stays Red* (London 1948) for a full account of the rent strikes in Stepney from 1937 onwards, in which the Communist Party took an active organizing role and was thereby able to check the drift among some tenants towards the British Union of Fascists.